Pastability

A Second Helping

Lizzie Spender

*Illustrations by
Karen Kerridge*

faber and faber
LONDON · BOSTON

First published in 1991 by
Faber and Faber Limited
3 Queen Square London WC1N 3AU

Photoset by Wilmaset, Birkenhead, Wirral
Printed in Great Britain by Clays Ltd St Ives plc

All rights reserved

© Lizzie Spender, 1991

Lizzie Spender is hereby identified as author of this work in accordance
with Section 77 of the Copyright, Designs and Patents Act 1988.

*This book is sold subject to the condition that it shall not, by way of trade
or otherwise, be lent, resold, hired out or otherwise circulated without the
publisher's prior consent in any form of binding or cover other than that
in which it is published and without a similar condition including
this condition being imposed on the subsequent purchaser.*

A CIP record for this book is available from the British Library.

ISBN 0-571-14431-4

For Stephen and Natasha Spender

Contents

Fish and meat – quick and easy

More fish, chicken and meat

Oriental – quick and easy

Oriental – fish, chicken and meat

Oriental – vegetarian

Acknowledgements

I would like to thank all those generous friends who have
provided me with encouragement, recipes, and inspiration for
my second cookery book. I have mentioned many of them in
the recipe introductions, but there are a few who for one
reason or another slipped through the net: Sandy Molloy,
Natasha Spender, and Tessa Humphries; Franco de Tommaso
from my local Italian delicatessen, La Solumeria, in St John's
Wood, London; Simon Hopkinson, the brilliant chef from the
Bibendum restaurant in London; Alfiero Centamore from
Coco's restaurant in Manchester; Teutonic culinary guru Wolf
Vecker; the Marchese Franco Sersale, the owner of the
legendary Le Syranuse Hotel in Positano; Sam and Angelo
from La Marina in Port Douglas, Queensland, Australia; Mario
Alfiero who owns a chain of restaurants in Surfer's Paradise on
the Gold Coast in Australia; and Giovanna Toppi of La Strada
in Sydney (although I *have* written about the restaurant which
she gave to her daughters – Machiavelli).

Last but not least, my husband Barry Humphries, who has
an inventive talent for piquant combinations. He always eats
pasta before his marathon one-man stage shows, and swears
that it is the pasta which gives him the energy for the second
act.

Foreword

THE PASTA DIET – STAMINA, WEIGHT LOSS AND HEALTH

I once knew an extremely beautiful and slim American lady who claimed that she put on weight if she did *not* eat pasta, suggesting that it was only when meat came into the house that her waistline thickened. I assumed that this was the kind of crazy assertion that only a naturally skinny person could afford to make, but in fact the changing attitudes to nutrition are bearing out her statement.

In my view pasta is the best 'weight-loss' food you can find. And the reasons are simple. Not only is it healthy and nutritious, but it is also now recognized as being the great new stamina food, and is frequently eaten by athletes and by marathon runners before a race. Pasta is a complex carbohydrate food and so even a small quantity provides the body with a steady and sustained flow of energy over an extended period of time. This energy gives the would-be dieter 'will power' because it keeps at bay the sudden hungers and energy lows which cause us to eat too much.

When the blood sugar level in your body falls, you naturally crave food to restore it, and in many cases we temporarily satisfy this craving with sugar, but sugar is the worst possible thing to eat because it is closer to a drug than a food and has no nutritional value whatsoever. It creates a false sugar 'high', at which point the body stops making its own sugar, so when the effect of the consumed sugar has worn off, the body is left with a 'low' and a craving for more.

Fat is also the enemy of the dieter. We all know about the evils of animal fats; not only are they high in calories but they also clog up the arteries. Unfortunately, even the olive and other vegetable and nut oils, although considerably better for you, are equally high in calories. Butter, olive oil, nut, seed, vegetable oils and even margarine all contain 100 calories per tablespoon (15 ml spoon), which is why you will find that I am extremely sparing with them in my recipes! I know that a lot of modern diets claim that calories are not the point. Personally, I don't believe them. Pasta on its own is not highly calorific –

only about 100 calories an ounce (25 g) when weighed uncooked and 33 calories an ounce when cooked – but of course, it all depends what you eat with or on it.

An ideal health and/or weight-loss diet contains a little pasta (even if only a couple of ounces) once or twice a day for energy and 'will power', with a low-fat sauce on the pasta for flavour and a large quantity of steamed, stir-fried or raw vegetables for fibre, vitamins and amino acids. Most vegetables, especially the green ones, are extremely low in calories; fruits are higher. For the non-vegetarians I would suggest some fish, chicken or cheese, or maybe even a little red meat for protein. Vegans and vegetarians have to balance their diets carefully to provide themselves with the necessary proteins, although good dried pasta made from durum wheat actually has a comparatively high percentage of protein: 13 to 16 per cent, against the 10 per cent to be found in bread flours.

There was a time when the optimum 'healthy' diet consisted of substantial intakes of animal proteins and fats, not to mention the obligatory 'pint of milk a day'. How else were we to form strong teeth and bones and keep them healthy but by consuming proteins direct from other animals?

Things have changed since then, however, and now most animal products are viewed with suspicion. I don't think there is anything wrong with a little meat, and if you occasionally feel like eating some, it could well mean that your body needs it. I don't believe we have all evolved to the point where we don't need any animal protein at all. In my view the safest and healthiest approach to good diet is to eat moderately of a good variety of different foods.

Lizzie Spender
December 1990

Introduction

TYPES AND SHAPES OF PASTA

There is an Italian name for every pasta shape and type, but only a few of these names are widely used outside Italy. To avoid confusion, and to help make shopping for pasta problem-free, I have used the Italian name only if a pasta is generally known by that name (e.g. tagliatelle). Otherwise, for pastas you would usually buy under an English name (e.g. shells), I have given the English names in the recipes.

The following is a list of the pastas I have used in this book with their Italian names and English equivalents where appropriate, and is included as a guide should you come across the Italian for a pasta which I have named in English.

Italian	English
cannelloni	
conchiglie	shells
farfalle	bows, butterflies
fettuccine	ribbon noodles
fusilli	twists
lasagne	
linguini	
maccheroni	macaroni, pasta tubes
penne	quills
rigatoni	ribbed pasta tubes
spaghetti	
spaghettini	
tagliatelle	ribbon noodles

HOW TO COOK PASTA

How much to cook?

A case of 'how long is a piece of string'! I have tried to give guides in each recipe of the appropriate quantities, but the appetites of guests and also how many other dishes and courses you are serving must be taken into account. A very rough thumbnail guide would be 1½–2 ounces (50 grammes) per person as a starter, or 3–4 ounces (75–125 grammes) per person as a main course. Bear in mind that the larger, heavier pasta shapes will appear to be a smaller serving when cooked than the same weight of smaller, lighter pasta.

How much water?

It is essential to cook the pasta in *plenty* of boiling water, otherwise it becomes sticky, soft and glutinous on the outside while still not properly cooked on the inside. You will need enough water for the pasta to move very freely, even when expanded towards the end of cooking, and if you can see the starch in the water (it will become slightly cloudy) then quickly boil a kettle and add more. I recommend using the following table as a guideline.

Pasta		*Water*	
ounces	grammes	pints	litres
Up to 4 oz	Up to 125 g	1½–2	1
4	125	2	1–1½
8	225	4	2½
16	450	8	4½
24	675	12	7
32	900	16	9

I possess one medium-size pan (4 pints) in which I cook 1–2 main course servings, and a couple of huge pans (16 pints) in which I cook larger quantities using whatever quantity of water is necessary.

To cook the pasta

It really hardly matters what sauce you put on your pasta – open your fridge door and be inventive – but what is absolutely essential is that you use the right sort of pasta and cook it the classical Italian way, using enough water, and taking it off the heat and draining at the 'al dente' stage.

First add to the water 1 teaspoon (1 × 5 ml spoon) of salt per

4 oz (100–125 g) pasta and $\frac{1}{2}$–1 teaspoon ($\frac{1}{2}$–1 × 5 ml spoon) oil – cheap vegetable oil will do. Bring the water to a fast boil before adding the pasta, otherwise you will increase the tendency for the pieces to stick together. Throw in the pasta *all at once*, and immediately stir well with a wooden spoon to separate the pieces. It is at this point that the pasta is in danger of congealing, so make sure the pieces are moving freely.

Cook until 'al dente', that is, done but still firm (not hard) to the bite. It takes practice to know when pasta is ready. Even now, I still almost always ask for a second opinion. It is almost impossible to predict how long a particular pasta will take to cook, which is why I have not given cooking times in the recipes. Thick, solid pieces, such as large pasta tubes or shells, will obviously take much longer than a fine spaghetti, but it is very dangerous to try to invent any rules of thumb as there are too many variables. Don't rely on the packet to give you the correct cooking time. Getting it right is really a matter of standing over the pan and, when the pasta is nearly ready, tasting every 45 seconds until it is. Pasta can overcook in just a matter of seconds, especially one that is not made from 100 per cent durum wheat semolina. I do *not* believe the old adage 'Throw a piece of spaghetti at the wall and if it sticks the pasta is ready.' In my experience, it all depends on how sticky your kitchen walls are!

When the pasta is 'al dente', drain it immediately into a colander standing in the sink. Then pick up the colander with its contents and shake it well to remove excess water before returning the pasta to the saucepan or a preheated serving dish.

I like to put the sauce and the pasta back in a pan over a low flame. I do this to ensure that the sauce is well integrated with the pasta and that the dish is served piping hot. Italians consider this to be rather sacrilegious; they prefer to mix the pasta with the sauce in the serving dish.

For the Oriental noodles, follow the instructions in the recipes, remembering that the Chinese egg noodles need cook for only a couple of minutes, and the cellophane noodles for literally seconds.

Timing your cooking

For most dishes the pasta and the sauce should be cooked simultaneously, so that the pasta is ready with the sauce. You will soon learn how to synchronize them, but don't despair if you don't. For most dishes it is possible to keep the sauce waiting as long as it is reheated gently while you are draining the pasta – and is served hot. If the pasta is cooked before you are ready to mix in the sauce, stir in a teaspoon of olive oil or a knob of butter. Mix in the sauce as soon as possible and serve immediately.

Aim to time your cooking so that the sauce is ready a little before the pasta. If you do find yourself in trouble, and the pasta has to wait, then throw a little oil on the drained pasta and reheat it *with the sauce*.

Occasionally, especially when entertaining friends, you may prefer to make the sauce well in advance. Reheat gently, and bear in mind you may need to add a little more liquid at the last minute.

Precooking lasagne and cannelloni

Cooking lasagne and cannelloni tubes is tricky. It's very easy to end up with burnt fingers and the pasta on the floor, or with a mass of congealed lasagne leaves impossible to separate. Many people swear by the 'oven-ready' type, although a few are brave enough to use the traditional kind without precooking. When I have tried this it has always been slightly too glutinous for my taste, and has taken a *long* time to cook in the oven.

To precook lasagne and cannelloni (my method)

First fill a large saucepan with 3–4 inches (8–10 cm) of water, and add ½ teaspoon (1 × 2.5 ml spoon) salt and ½ teaspoon (1 × 2.5 ml spoon) oil. Bring the water to a fast boil before slipping in the lasagne leaves (or cannelloni tubes) three at a time, stirring well with a wooden spoon to separate them. After 2–3 minutes, when the pasta is still very 'al dente' (i.e. slightly undercooked), remove the pieces one by one using a slotted spoon and the wooden spoon – and taking care not to let the pasta slip out of your grip! Dip each leaf or tube into a shallow bowl containing cold water and a couple of

4

tablespoons of oil. Then put to one side on a board, spread out and overlapped like a deck of cards.

I have found the best way to make lasagne or cannelloni dishes is to prepare the sauce before cooking the pasta. I can then lay the precooked pasta in the baking dish as soon as it is removed from the boiling water, adding the sauce as I go. This method avoids all the fiddly business of rinsing the pasta in cold water and spreading it on a flat surface.

FRESH PASTA

As I said in *Pastability*, I hardly ever use fresh pasta. I would be the first to say 'fresh is best', but unfortunately this is usually not the case for pasta. Most of the products available from Italy are vastly inferior to the better brands of dried pasta, such as F.lli de Cecco and Barilla, and sadly in my experience that also goes for the pasta made in your own home.

What never ceases to amaze me is the blind faith with which 'fresh' pasta is proudly served in this country on the assumption that as it is 'fresh' and more expensive it just *has* to be better, when the truth of it is that on the plate in front of me I find either a barely disguised quantity of indigestible, undercooked flour and water dough, or an overcooked soggy mass. Yes, I'm exaggerating, but either way it sits in the stomach like a lead balloon! Of course, if you find a local shop that supplies a wonderful fresh pasta, easy to cook and serve and simply delicious, then who am I to argue with that? However, my advice is to steer well clear of the so-called 'fresh' pasta found on the cold shelves in supermarkets, much of which is actually pasteurized. In Italy fresh pasta is not often served in either private houses or restaurants (except to tourists), so why are we so hooked on it here?

There was an aristocratic lady living in Milan in the 1930s who was famous for the marvellous fresh pasta served at her table. Nobody could discover the secret, least of all the lady herself, until one day, walking unannounced into her kitchen, the truth was revealed. Her chef was rolling out the pasta against his bare and sweating chest!

As I said before, the best pasta is made from durum (hard) wheat flour, which contains 13–16 per cent protein, as opposed to the 10 per cent to be found in bread flour. The big pasta companies buy up the wheat before it is even harvested. I'm told De Cecco buy their wheat from California, which might explain why their pasta seems to grow to about two or three times its original size while cooking! Good-quality durum wheat flour is almost impossible to buy in Britain, so most fresh pasta is made from the low-protein bread farine. It is the protein content in the flour which gives the pasta the characteristic springy, slightly chewy quality it has when cooked to the 'al dente' stage. The problem with fresh or dried pasta made without this high-protein flour is that it appears to pass from raw and undercooked to soft and slightly mushy with no intervening 'al dente' stage, and so not only is less appetizing to eat, but also cannot be eaten later, reheated or eaten cold.

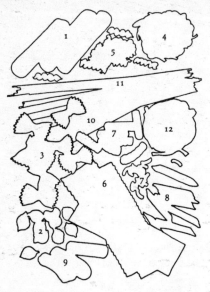

1 cannelloni	7 marcaroni
2 conchiglie	8 penne
3 farfalle	9 rigatoni
4 fettuccine	10 spaghetti
5 fusilli	11 spaghettini
6 lasagne	12 tagliatelle

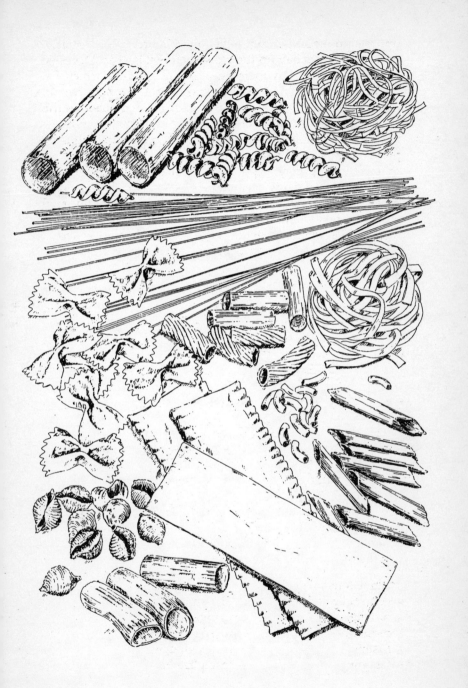

Storing and cooking fresh pasta

Genuine fresh pasta keeps in the fridge for two or three days. It is possible to freeze it – in which case it keeps for up to six months – and to cook it directly from the freezer. For tagliatelle or spaghetti I would recommend the following method of freezing. Spread the pasta out flat on a plate (or plates) to a thickness of not more than an inch or so (about 3 cm). Put the plate and pasta into a plastic bag and freeze. When the pasta is frozen, remove the plate, seal the pasta into the plastic bag, and return it to the deep freeze. If you freeze the pasta as a solid mass in a bag, when the time comes to cook it there is a danger the outside strands will be 'al dente' while the centre of the lump is still completely frozen.

Fresh pasta takes considerably less time to cook than dried. It is dangerous to try to predict how long, as all pasta is different. Count on a third to a half of the time the equivalent dried pasta would take – usually less than 3 minutes, and a maximum of 5. Watch it like a hawk as it can overcook in a matter of seconds.

WHICH TYPE OF PASTA?

The types of pasta I have suggested are those which are most readily available in the shops, and for each recipe I have suggested a type or types I know from experience will go well with that particular sauce. Of course, you do not have to use the pasta I have specified – you can substitute one type for another according to your own preference and what is to hand.

With Italian cooking there are traditional combinations of pasta type and sauce which are probably more consistently adhered to in restaurants than in private houses. There are also theories which I have heard discussed more frequently in America than in Italy: that the simple oil sauce clings best to the pasta strand, such as spaghetti and linguini; that the shell-like shapes scoop up a semi-liquid sauce; that the meat with oil sauce – the bolognese ragù – sticks to the ridges of the ribbed, tubular rigatoni. The twists, I suppose, do a bit of everything. Remember that a heavy pasta is the best complement to a heavy sauce.

8

HOW TO SERVE PASTA

It is essential with most pasta dishes that they be served *very* hot, and as soon as they are ready. It is therefore advisable to round up those about to eat the pasta and persuade them to sit at the table just *before* the dish is actually ready! Plates should be well warmed in advance, and it is important, if you are intending to transfer the pasta from the pan to a serving dish, to preheat the dish too.

I do abhor the habit of dolloping grated cheese on to every kind of pasta *before* tasting and deciding whether or not this particular dish would be improved by the taste of Parmesan, or Cheddar, or whichever cheese you are offering. Please try to persuade your guests to taste first!

ORIENTAL PASTA

In my first book, *Pastability*, I used only Italian pastas, but in this book I have broadened my horizons and used a couple of basic Chinese and Oriental noodles.

Chinese egg noodles

Thin, brittle, yellow noodles, dried in 5-inch (13-cm) looped skeins. Sold in packets in Chinese and Oriental provision shops, and some supermarkets. You can substitute a fine Italian egg pasta, a 'vermicelli' or 'angel hair'. F.lli de Cecco do an excellent box of little 'birds' nests' of vermicelli, but use the Chinese noodles if you can.

Cellophane noodles or 'vermicelli' (Thai name: Wun Sen)

Fine noodles made from the starch of green mung beans. Sometimes known as 'glass' noodles. As the name suggests, they are transparent. They are soaked in cold water for 20 minutes, and then dunked in boiling water for just 30 seconds. Available as above. Do not be put off by their rather slippery texture and taste. You will quickly grow to love them.

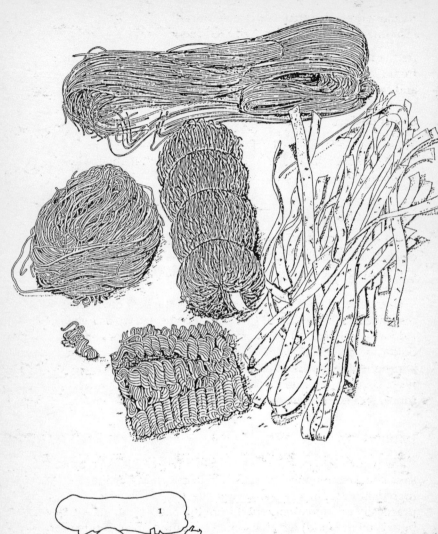

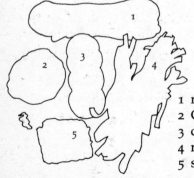

1 rice vermicelli
2 Chinese egg noodles
3 cellophane noodles or vermicelli
4 rice sticks
5 soba noodles

Rice noodles, rice sticks or rice vermicelli
(Thai names: Sen Yai, Sen Lek, Sen Mee)

As the names suggest, noodles in different sizes but all made from rice. Again these noodles are soaked for 20–30 minutes and then dropped for less than a minute into boiling water.

Soba noodles

These are the Japanese 'buckwheat' noodles, available in Japanese supermarkets. You can always substitute buckwheat noodles from your health-food shop.

LEFTOVERS

Make the most of leftovers – cold vegetables, scraps of meat or chicken, ends of cheese, sauces from stews and casseroles. All can be utilized in the concoction of delicious, original pasta sauces.

Leftover cold pasta can always be used the next day. Some dishes taste excellent cold. Others can be heated up as follows. Add a little liquid – chicken stock, cream, white wine, oil, butter, or combinations of these – and warm gently in a pan, stirring with a wooden spoon and adding more liquid if necessary. Another possibility is to mix in some béchamel sauce, sprinkle grated cheese on top and bake in the oven.

IMPROVISATION

Allow yourself to be led by your taste buds, and make a pasta sauce out of anything that strikes your fancy! My recipe ingredients are, in a sense, only suggestions. There is practically no ingredient (apart from the pasta itself and a little butter, oil or liquid) which cannot be omitted or substituted for another. I make pasta sauces with whatever I find in the fridge or larder, or whatever looks fresh and is a good buy in the shops. I consider it a creative challenge to be presented with somebody else's fridge or cupboard – however bare – and asked to concoct a pasta dish.

STANDBY INGREDIENTS

If you keep a selection of dried pastas and some basic sauce ingredients you will be able to throw together a pasta meal at short notice and without a quick dash to the shops. The following list includes all the basic standbys, with items I regard as absolutely essential marked with an asterisk.

The storecupboard

*tinned Italian plum tomatoes (Ciro is recommended by my Italian friends, but Waitrose, Safeway's and Sainsbury's brands are also good)
*tomato purée (available in tubes, jars, tins or cartons to be kept in the fridge once opened. Transfer remaining contents of a tin to another receptacle)
tins of fish: *anchovies; salmon; sardines; *tuna fish; clams; crab; mussels (but not those preserved in a vinegary liquid)
olives and capers
*chicken stock cubes (or vegetable cubes if you are vegetarian)
*garlic
dried red chillies; chilli powder
*dried herbs (especially marjoram, oregano, sage, thyme, basil)
*sea salt
*whole black peppercorns
longlife cream
pesto sauce (the jar should be kept in the fridge after it has been opened)
wine
*good olive oil   It is essential to use a top-quality olive oil. Luckily the big supermarket chains have finally woken up to the importance of decent olive oil, and most of them stock a good selection at reasonable prices.
*vegetable or nut oil   The Oriental dishes require an oil without flavour – something simple like sunflower or safflower. Never use olive oil in Oriental dishes. However, a few drops of sesame oil can impart a very appropriate and delicious taste. Be guided by your taste buds.
*pasta   A selection of packets of your favourite brand of pasta, in different shapes and types. I prefer the make F.lli de Cecco di Filippo, recognizable by its bright turquoise and yellow packets. It is available in Italian delicatessens, and I

make a point of stocking up whenever I find it. I also use and highly recommend Barilla, which is more easily available. Whatever the brand, always use a pasta which is made from 100 per cent durum wheat semolina. It will not only be more nutritious than a pasta made with a softer flour, or a mixture of flours, but will also be easier to cook. It will remain at the 'al dente' stage for a little longer, thus lessening the hazard of your perfectly cooked pasta turning into a congealed and soggy mess somewhere between draining and serving.

The fridge

eggs
single and double cream
*butter
bacon
fresh vegetables
*fresh, ungrated Parmesan cheese and/or fresh Cheddar
  cheese
*onions   Do experiment with the unusual varieties if you
  come across them – the little shallots for example, or the
  large, dark-red onion.

The freezer

If you have a freezer, I would recommend storing a selection of the following items:
  chicken breasts
  chicken livers
  minced meat
  prawns
  leaf spinach
  peas
  broad beans

Parmesan cheese

Parmesan is best bought in a lump and kept wrapped in paper in the fridge. It must not be covered in clingfilm or foil: if it cannot breathe it will go mouldy. Stored this way the cheese should keep for months, so it is well worth buying a decent-sized piece when the opportunity arises. Buying Parmesan can be a painful experience, for it is expensive. Console yourself with the fact that a little goes a long way. It is *not* worth bothering with the little packets and round boxes of ready-grated Parmesan: the stuff is tasteless and expensive – and does *not* go a long way.

Grate the Parmesan as and when you need it. Quite often I leave a lump of Parmesan with a grater on a plate on the table. This is not only economical, but it discourages people from the deplorable habit of throwing a spoon of Parmesan on to the pasta before they have tasted the dish and decided whether or not that particular dish needs it. Parmesan has a strong flavour and can drown the delicate taste of some dishes.

ORIENTAL INGREDIENTS

Nowadays, the basics of Oriental cooking are widely available in most parts of the world. However, there are ingredients which are essential in the preparation of Thai food which seem to be obtainable only in Thai provision shops. Once you have the ingredients at hand, Thai dishes are on the whole very simple and quick to prepare, and a trip to a Thai shop is always fun providing you go armed with a list of the essential ingredients you require. Here is a list of the basic Oriental necessities. Check first with the recipes you are intending to make to find out your exact requirements. The asterisks denote Thai ingredients available, in my experience, only in Thai shops – the rest you can find in supermarkets or local Oriental provision stores, of which there seems to be a constantly growing number in all parts of the world.

Aubergine   Some Oriental shops stock a very nice aubergine, about an inch or two in diameter and green in colour. If you can't get hold of any, then substitute the usual purple/black variety.
*Basil, holy   Not quite like the basil the Italians use. The leaves are darker and smaller, and the taste not quite so sweet.
Bean curd (tofu)   Very nutritious and non-fattening, with a bland taste which grows on you. Nowadays available all

over the place. The firmer the better. Keeps for a couple of
days in the fridge.

Chillies   Can be bought fresh, red or green. I usually use the
dried red variety, which are mega-strong! Be careful never to
wipe your eyes after handling one. Can substitute chilli
powder or chilli oil.

Black bean sauce   Useful. Again, read the label with care and
avoid the ones with monosodium glutamate.

Coconut milk   Bears as little resemblance to the stuff inside
the coconut you win at a funfair as skimmed milk does to
condensed milk. It took me years to get to grips with this
one! I used to try melting down bars of solid coconut cream,
and manufacturing coconut milk out of desiccated coconut
and milk, and the conclusion I have come to is that there is
no substitute for a decent tin of the stuff. I buy Chaokrung
coconut milk from the Thai shop. Remember that, as with
full-cream milk, the cream and the milk separate so you
must decant the whole can into a bowl and beat with a fork.
Once opened it keeps in the fridge, but not for long. Any
coconut milk left over can be frozen for next time.

*Curry paste   One of the great joys of the Thai food stores,
apart from the charming Thais who work in them, is that
they stock the basic curry pastes ready made up. In my local
shop it is possible to buy them in handy-sized plastic
sachets. In this book I have used three: green curry paste,
red curry paste and matsaman curry paste. Keeps in the
fridge, but make sure you put it in a sturdy airtight
container.

Coriander, fresh leaves   Available nowadays in more and
more shops. Even the big supermarkets stock it. Absolutely
delicious and a must for Oriental cooking. Try it in salads.

Cardamom pods   Little grey-green husky pods. Inside are the
most delicious black seeds. Available from supermarkets.

Dried shrimp   I usually pick up a small packet when I'm in
the Thai shop.

Fish sauce, fish gravy   You don't need a lot of this. In fact, I
think most Thai restaurants in this country use a bit too
much for our Western palates, unaccustomed as we are to
fermented fish gravy, either in theory or in practice. The first
time I ever cooked with it I panicked and threw the contents
of the pan down the sink, fearing that it would irrevocably

taint my precious saucepan. But I have found that by buying a fairly innocuous variety, the colour and consistency of a good brandy, and using it in moderation, it is a valuable addition to Oriental cooking.

Galangal (or kha)   Very useful for the Thai coconut curries. Looks a bit like ginger root.

Garlic

Ginger   Fresh ginger root, nowadays available almost everywhere and an essential ingredient in Oriental cooking of all kinds.

Lemon grass   Available in some forward-thinking supermarkets, and, of course, at the Thai shop, in the form of stalks or a kind of giant grass. The flavour is very characteristic of Thai cooking.

*Lime leaves (also known as citrus leaves, or kaffir lime leaves)   In my view, the very powerful flavour of these leaves is the key to Thai cuisine. Buy them in packets only at the Thai shop, and keep them in the fridge well wrapped up or else the strong flavour will taint other items of food. If you are keeping them more than a few days, freeze them. Cut them with kitchen scissors.

Oil   Oriental dishes require an oil without flavour – something simple like sunflower or safflower. Never use olive oil in Oriental dishes. However, a few drops of sesame oil can impart an appropriate and delicious taste.

Palm sugar   Available in Oriental shops. I sometimes substitute a thick, tasteless honey, or black sugar.

Peanuts   Avoid the salted cocktail variety. Thai shops do a bag of raw peanuts, which I then roast in a pan in the oven. To crush, put them in a plastic bag and beat with a rolling pin.

Soy sauce   Of course, an essential part of Oriental cuisine. Beware of the cheap imitations containing strange substances and monosodium glutamate. I buy Kikkoman, which is a Japanese product.

Spring onion   Seems to appear in Oriental recipes almost as frequently as garlic.

EQUIPMENT

The essential basic equipment for cooking pasta dishes is minimal. A large saucepan in which to cook the pasta itself (*very* large if you are intending to entertain more than four or five people), and a large colander for draining it; a medium-sized frying pan and medium-sized saucepan for preparing sauces; a couple of wooden spoons for stirring (and possibly serving) the pasta and sauce; a large bowl or plate, which can be preheated, for serving the pasta at table; a couple of ovenproof dishes or pans for cooking lasagne and other baked pasta dishes; and a cheese grater, a garlic squeezer and a sharp knife for chopping meat and vegetables.

For the Oriental dishes there is no doubt that a wok is extremely useful. If you don't have one, put it on your Christmas/birthday list instantly! With the wok will probably come a large wooden spatula for stir frying, although you can also use a wooden spoon. A sharp knife is very helpful for all the fine chopping, and personally I like to eat all Oriental food with chopsticks.

METRIC WEIGHTS AND MEASURES

In all the recipes I have given both imperial and metric weights and measures – but not in exact conversions. Rather, for ease of measuring in grammes and millilitres, I have given conversions from imperial to metric in units of 25. Where an exact conversion lies midway between two such units, I have indicated this by giving the units below and above the precise conversion. *For example*: 3 ounces converts to approximately 85 grammes, and would be shown as 75–100 grammes in the recipes.

The one exception of this principle is ½ ounce, which throughout has been given as 15 grammes.

BECHAMEL SAUCE

Béchamel sauce is used in a number of the recipes. Rather than repeat the instructions for making it each time it occurs, I have given the basic recipe at the end of the book (page 169) and included the quantities needed for individual recipes in the ingredients lists.

CHICKEN STOCK

Chicken stock really is invaluable in the cooking of pasta sauces, especially Oriental ones. It is worth boiling up the bones whenever you have chicken and storing the stock in a condensed form in the deep freeze. Boil it until it is very condensed, and then freeze in an ice tray, decanting the iced stock cubes into a plastic bag for future use. Again, I have given the basic recipe on page 81 (Chicken noodle soup).

SYMBOLS

♡ I have marked this symbol next to those recipes which I would consider most suitable for people eager to follow a good diet for a healthy heart. It goes without saying that I am not a doctor, and anyone with heart problems should consult their physician for dietary recommendations.

○ I have marked this symbol next to those recipes which I consider most suitable for people attempting to lose weight. These dishes can help you to lose weight only as part of a calorie-controlled diet – in other words, only if eaten in small quantities in conjunction with other low-calorie foods.

Vegetarian dishes – quick and easy

Spaghetti with tarragon and lemon   ♡ ○

It goes without saying that you must decide you like the taste
of tarragon before trying this dish. A good light lunch dish,
especially good after a too-late and too-rich supper the night
before. There are two versions really – with just the grated
lemon rind, or with the addition of lemon juice and Parmesan
(the lemon juice is a little strong on its own, but the Parmesan
cancels that out). I would recommend spaghetti or spaghettini.

For 2 light helpings, use:

> 1½ tablespoons (1½ × 15 ml spoons) good olive oil
> 3 tablespoons (3 × 15 ml spoons) fresh tarragon, coarsely
>   chopped or torn up with your fingers
> grated rind 1 lemon
> 1 tablespoon (1 × 15 ml spoon) freshly squeezed lemon
>   juice (optional)
> 1 tablespoon (1 × 15 ml spoon) freshly grated Italian
>   Parmesan, or more, to taste (optional)
> 5–6 oz (150–175 g) spaghetti or spaghettini

Cook the pasta in plenty of salted boiling water until 'al
dente'. Drain, and put back into the pan with the oil, grated
lemon rind and tarragon. Toss, then add the lemon juice if
using and toss again. Serve on preheated plates with the
Parmesan cheese – if using – on the side, or sprinkled on top.

Shells with soft blue cheese, cottage cheese and olives

There are so many blue cheeses on the market nowadays – experiment with whatever looks like a good buy at your local shops. Serve with a big mixed salad, including watercress, grated carrot and raw mushrooms.

For 2 main course or 4 starter helpings, use:

> 4 oz (100–125 g) cottage cheese
> 4 oz (100–125 g) soft blue cheese
> 8 large black olives (pitted and cut into quarters)
> freshly ground black pepper
> 6–8 oz (175–225 g) pasta shells or quills

Crumble or chop the blue cheese into small pieces and mix together with the cottage cheese. Meanwhile, cook the pasta in plenty of salted, boiling water until 'al dente', drain, and put back into the pan. Add the cheese mixture and heat through over a low flame, stirring constantly until the cheese has melted and evenly coated the pasta. Sprinkle over the chopped olives and serve immediately, piping hot, with plenty of freshly ground black pepper on the side.

Bows with pesto, pine kernels, sun-dried tomatoes and Ricotta

Some of the best recipes invent themselves when you are hungry, in a hurry and just throwing in whichever ingredients come to hand! Under these circumstances the worst failures can happen too, but on the whole, hunger and greed are pretty reliable and creative driving forces!

This recipe was invented in a hurry – I had just bought some Ricotta cheese but the other ingredients were straight out of the storecupboard. If you have no Ricotta, I would be inclined to just leave it out rather than substitute any other cheese – there's nothing *quite* like it. The pesto sauce was bottled and out of my larder – as I said in *Pastability*, it is difficult to find fresh basil in Britain to make your own, so I tend to rely on bottled and spruce it up with extra garlic and oil.

For 2 light main course helpings, use:

1½ tablespoons (1½ × 15 ml spoons) bottled pesto sauce
1½ tablespoons (1½ × 15 ml spoons) olive oil
1–2 cloves garlic, crushed
1½ tablespoons (1½ × 15 ml spoons) pine kernels
2–3 sun-dried tomatoes, chopped
2 oz (50 g) Ricotta cheese
5–6 oz (150–175 g) pasta bows or butterflies
fresh Parmesan cheese (if not available substitute another hard cheese)
freshly ground black pepper

In the bottom of a medium to small pan, mix together the pesto, olive oil, garlic, pine kernels and sun-dried tomatoes. Warm slightly just before adding to the pasta. Put the Ricotta on to a plate and break up with a fork.

Cook the pasta in plenty of salted boiling water until 'al dente', drain, and put into the pan with the sauce over a low flame. Mix together well, and then throw on the Ricotta cheese and toss together. Serve immediately with plenty of freshly ground pepper and fresh Parmesan cheese on the side.

Spaghetti with hard-boiled eggs, parsley and garlic

A very quick and easy but tasty dish. Feel free to use more garlic.

For 2 light main course helpings, use:

> 2 eggs, hard boiled
> 4 tablespoons (4 × 15 ml spoons) olive oil
> 2–3 cloves garlic, crushed
> 4 tablespoons (4 × 15 ml spoons) parsley, finely chopped
> 6 oz (175 g) spaghetti
> sea salt and freshly ground black pepper
> freshly grated Parmesan cheese, *or* substitute 1 tablespoon
>   (1 × 15 ml spoon) of chopped capers*

Peel the eggs, then put them on a plate and mash with a fork. Measure the oil into a cup, then add the mashed eggs, garlic and finely chopped parsley.

Meanwhile, cook the pasta in plenty of salted boiling water until 'al dente'. Drain and return to the pan. Pour over the sauce, seasoning and the freshly grated Parmesan or chopped capers. Serve immediately with more Parmesan on the side.

---

* The capers provide an interestingly tangy alternative to the Parmesan.

Spaghettini with oyster mushrooms, garlic and parsley   ♡ ○

'Exotic' ingredients such as oyster mushrooms are now far more widely available, but if they are not for sale in your local shops you could always make this dish using ordinary mushrooms – if possible the open flat 'field' variety; they're tastier than the crisp white button sort.

You can also make this recipe leaving out the wine.

For 2 main course or 4 starter helpings, use:

 3 tablespoons (3 × 15 ml spoons) olive oil
 2 cloves garlic, crushed
 8 oz (225 g) oyster mushrooms, finely sliced
 3 tablespoons (3 × 15 ml spoons) parsley, finely chopped
    or 3 teaspoons (3 × 5 ml spoons) dried oregano
 3 tablespoons (3 × 15 ml spoons) white wine (optional)
 salt and pepper
 7 oz (200 g) spaghettini or spaghetti

Add the crushed garlic to 2 tablespoons (2 × 15 ml spoons) of the oil, and heat gently. Throw in the mushrooms and sauté for a minute or two. Add the white wine, if you are using it, and sauté for another couple of minutes. The parsley or oregano and seasoning should be added to the sauce at the last moment.

Meanwhile, cook the pasta in plenty of salted boiling water until 'al dente'. Drain, and put back into the pan. Pour on the remaining tablespoon (15 ml spoon) olive oil and mix well with a wooden spoon so that all the pasta has a fine coating of oil. Add the sauce, mix, and serve immediately, piping hot, with or without freshly grated Parmesan cheese on the side.

Bows with mashed courgettes, Parmesan and basil

♡ ○

This recipe was given to me by Mariluis Pallavicino, an Italian friend. She insists that this dish should be made with neither chilli nor garlic but, addict that I am, I cannot resist adding a smidgen of both. If basil is not available then simply make the dish without it, and you can substitute marrow or even broccoli for the courgettes.

A light and refreshing dish, but if you crave something spicier then mash in a couple of anchovy fillets (♡ omit anchovies).

For 2 light main course helpings, use:

> 10 oz (275 g) courgettes, sliced
> 1 oz (25 g) Parmesan cheese, medium grated
> 1 tablespoon (1 × 15 ml spoon) olive oil
> 1 clove garlic, crushed (optional)
> 1 very small dried red chilli, crumbled (optional)
> 5 oz (150 g) pasta bows (or similar shapes)
> 5–10 leaves of fresh basil, torn into small pieces

Boil the courgettes in lightly salted water for at least 5 minutes, until soft. Put on a plate and mash with a fork. Stir in the oil and basil leaves, then the garlic, chilli and anchovy, if using; add two-thirds of the grated cheese.

Meanwhile, cook the pasta in plenty of well-salted boiling water until 'al dente', drain, and put back in the pan with the courgette mixture. Toss over a low flame for a couple of minutes until well mixed and heated through. Serve with the remaining cheese sprinkled on top, and with plenty of freshly ground black pepper.

Gian Carlo Menotti's 'spaghetti dei poveri' with tomatoes, parsley and garlic

This pasta sauce was invented in Naples during the Second World War at a time when meat was scarce. The flavour of the burnt garlic and the texture of the parsley give the impression of a 'ragù' or meat sauce.

The recipe was given to me by the great Italian composer Gian Carlo Menotti. He prepared it for us on a cold stormy night at his magnificent house in Scotland.

For 2 main course helpings, use:

> 6 tablespoons (6 × 15 ml spoons) olive oil
> 3 cloves garlic*
> 14 oz (400 g) tinned chopped tomatoes
> 2 oz (50 g) parsley, finely chopped
> 6 oz (175 g) spaghetti or spaghettini
> 1 fresh Italian Mozzarella (4–5 oz/100–150 g) chopped into small cubes (optional)

Sauté the sliced garlic in the hot oil (in a small pan with a lid) until well browned. Strain out the garlic, and put the oil back in the pan. Transfer the tinned tomatoes into a shallow bowl (a cereal bowl will do). Reheat the oil on a medium flame until very hot. Very quickly remove the lid, slide in the tomatoes and slam the lid back on immediately, taking care not to be burnt by the spitting hot oil. The tomatoes will cool down the oil considerably, so it will now be safe to add the parsley. Simmer on a fairly high flame for about 10 minutes, stirring occasionally and taking care not to let the sauce stick.

Meanwhile, cook the pasta in plenty of well-salted boiling water until 'al dente', drain, and put back in the pan with the

---

* Garlic addicts might like to consider recycling the garlic. In other words, slicing it before cooking, putting aside after straining the oil, then serving it sprinkled on top of the finished dish. You could also add a freshly squeezed clove to the sauce at the same time as adding the parsley.

tomato sauce. Add the chopped Mozzarella, if using, and then toss over a low flame for a couple of minutes until well mixed and heated through, when the Mozzarella should be nice and gooey. Serve immediately.

Gnocchetti* with spring greens, red pepper and Mozzarella ♡ ○

This recipe was given to me by an Italian friend (and brilliant cook), Emmalisa Marcozzi Rozzi. Emmalisa lives in London and cooks pasta regularly for her husband and their friends. She uses F.lli de Cecco pasta, or else buys it fresh from Harrods, and invents sauces out of locally available ingredients. Both the red pepper and the Mozzarella are optional additions to the original recipe.

For 3–4 light main course helpings, use:

1 lb (450 g) spring greens
3 tablespoons (3 × 15 ml spoons) olive oil
1–2 cloves garlic, crushed
1–2 small dried red chillies, crumbled or finely chopped
1 medium sweet red pepper, chopped
1 fresh Italian Mozzarella (4–5 oz/100–150 g), chopped into
  small cubes
(♡ ○ omit Mozzarella)
8 oz (225 g) gnocchetti, or other small pasta shapes

Slice the greens across into strips about ½ inch (1 cm) wide, then slice the other way across into small squares. Boil in lightly salted water for 8–10 minutes (depending on how tough the leaves are). Drain well, then put aside.

Sauté the chopped red pepper with the garlic and chillies in 2 tablespoons (2 × 15 ml spoons) of the oil until the pepper has softened. Add the cooked greens and sauté together for a couple of minutes.

Meanwhile, cook the pasta in plenty of well-salted boiling water until 'al dente'. Drain, and toss together with the remaining spoon of oil. Add the pasta and Mozzarella to the vegetable mixture, and heat through well on a medium flame until the dish is piping hot and the cheese pleasantly gooey. Serve immediately.

* Gnocchetti Sardi: a small pasta shape (¾ in/2 cm long) made by F.lli de Cecco, resembling a hollow caterpillar.

Twists with tomatoes and blue cheese

Use any blue cheese you like for this recipe: Gorgonzola, Stilton, Dolcelatte, or even a combination of leftover bits from the cheeseboard.

Serve with a mixed green salad including, if possible, watercress and/or raw spinach leaves.

For 2 main course helpings, use:

$\frac{1}{2}$ tablespoon ($\frac{1}{2}$ × 15 ml spoon) butter
6 oz (175 g) fresh ripe tomatoes
3 oz (75–100 g) blue cheese
4 tablespoons (4 × 15 ml spoons) single or double cream
6 oz (175 g) twists
fresh basil (if available)

Skin the tomatoes and then chop coarsely. (I find the best way to skin the tomatoes is to drop them into the boiling pasta water for a minute or so, before adding the pasta, then remove with a slotted spoon; the skin, which should already be broken, will slide off the tomatoes with the greatest of ease.) Break or chop the blue cheese into pea-size chunks and mix together with the cream.

Meanwhile, cook the pasta in plenty of salted boiling water until 'al dente'. Drain, and put back into the pan. Add the butter and chopped tomatoes, and heat gently over a low flame, stirring continuously, until the butter has melted and the tomatoes are evenly distributed. Add the blue cheese and cream, and continue to stir over a low heat until the cheese has completely melted and the pasta dish is well mixed and heated through. Sprinkle over with fresh basil leaves and serve immediately.

Spicy mayonnaise, hard-boiled egg and pasta shell salad

A good dish to serve as part of a summer lunch or buffet, this invention owes at least a little of its inspiration to the ubiquitous 'Coronation Chicken'. So if you have some leftover chicken in the fridge – throw it in as well.

Don't be put off by the inclusion of 'apricot jam' in this recipe – I can assure you that the end result really is good.

For 4–8 salad size helpings, use:

4 tablespoons (4 × 15 ml spoons) tomato juice
1 teaspoon (1 × 5 ml spoon) curry powder
2 teaspoons (2 × 5 ml spoons) apricot jam or marmalade
1½ tablespoons (1½ × 15 ml spoons) lemon juice
6 tablespoons (6 × 15 ml spoons) mayonnaise (I use
  Hellmann's)
8 oz (225 g) pasta shells or shapes
2 eggs, hard-boiled

Put the tomato juice, curry powder and marmalade or apricot jam into a small pan and heat gently, stirring continuously, for a couple of minutes until the curry powder has dissolved and the marmalade has melted. Continue to simmer for a couple more minutes – *very* gently, or it will reduce. Mix together with the mayonnaise and the lemon juice and then season to taste.

Meanwhile, cook the pasta in plenty of salted boiling water until 'al dente', drain, and toss together with the sauce while still warm. Slice the hard-boiled eggs and add to the pasta. Readjust seasoning if necessary. Chill.

Quills with carrots, olives and English cheese

A very simple and quick storecupboard standby. For a bit of extra bite, add a couple of dashes of Worcestershire or Tabasco sauce.

For 2 main course helpings, use:

> 8 oz (225 g) carrots
> 3 tablespoons (3 × 15 ml spoons) olive oil
> 6 oz (175 g) onion, finely sliced
> 8–10 black olives, pitted and chopped
> 3 oz (75–100 g) Lancashire cheese, grated (or substitute
>   Wensleydale or mild Cheddar)
> 6 oz (175 g) quills or shells

Steam or boil the carrots until softened but not mushy. Chop moderately finely. Sauté the onion in the oil until softened and translucent, stir in the carrot, season, and continue to sauté for about 5 minutes.

Meanwhile, cook the pasta in plenty of salted boiling water until softened and translucent. Drain, and put back into the pan. Add the carrot and onion, with the olives and the cheese, and heat through over a low heat, stirring continuously, until the cheese has melted. Serve immediately.

Kimberley spaghetti sandwiches

I first experienced this remarkably tasty dish in Australia. We had 'gone bush' for a few days and were staying with some friends, David and Susan Bradley, on their magnificent cattle station, Carlton Hill. This spectacular property in the Kimberleys – the 'outback' of North-west Australia – extends over a mere two million acres, stocks 40,000 head of cattle, and is one of the most beautiful and fascinating places I've ever seen.

Spaghetti sandwiches are consumed with gusto by the 'ringers' or 'jackaroos' (Australian version of cowboys) at 'smoko' (morning tea), served at 9.30 after the first few hours of 'mustering' (rounding up cattle). Extremely healthy appetites are ensured by the early start, which can mean anything between 3.00 am and 5.30 am, depending on the moon and the urgency of the task – for example, rescuing heifers stuck in the muddy river bank from being devoured by twelve-foot man-eating crocodiles! After such hungry work these sandwiches are always the first thing to go. Serve with strong tea out of a chipped enamel mug.

Allow two sandwiches per cowboy:

> 1 tin Heinz spaghetti
> Sliced white bread
> Lots of butter

Butter the bread, and then make the sandwiches, filling with the Heinz spaghetti. Fry on both sides in a large frying pan in more *hot* butter until golden. Serve immediately.

More vegetarian dishes

Pasta and vegetable soup ♡ ○

The delicious Italian minestrone soup has sadly been given a bad name due to the quite horrendous concoctions masquerading under that name in all too many cafés and restaurants – soft cubes of tasteless carrot, old peas and a few noodles swimming in a dishwater broth. A real minestrone is a feast of fresh vegetables, pasta and stock – a nourishing and filling meal in itself.

The following minestrone is one of my favourites. The bacon gives the dish quite a strong, smoky taste which I find totally delicious, though it does slightly dominate the flavour. You can leave out the bacon if you prefer. Similarly, if you don't have any of the vegetables listed, leave them out or substitute another fresh sliced or chopped vegetable, or include more of the vegetables you do have.

For 4 main course or 8 starter helpings, use:

2 tablespoons (2 × 15 ml spoons) olive oil
6 oz (175 g) onion, chopped
6 oz (175 g) leeks, sliced
3 cloves garlic, sliced or crushed
2 oz (50 g) smoked bacon, derinded and chopped
    (optional)
(♡ omit bacon)
6 oz (175 g) Savoy cabbage, finely sliced
4 oz (100–125 g) parsnips, sliced
6 oz (175 g) courgettes, sliced
6 oz (175 g) broccoli, sliced
6 oz (175 g) tomatoes, skinned and chopped
3 pints (1.7 litres) good fresh chicken or vegetable stock
3 bay leaves
salt and pepper
3–4 oz (75–125) pasta shapes (e.g. shells)
Parmesan cheese (fresh, or substitute another cheese such
    as Cheddar or Gruyère)
(♡ omit or go easy on the cheese)

Sauté the onions and leeks in the oil until softened and

translucent. Add the bacon and sauté for another couple of minutes. Prepare the vegetables as you go, adding them one at a time (leaving a couple of minutes between each new addition), and stirring frequently with a wooden spoon. Finally, add the stock, bay leaves, seasonings, and simmer on a low heat for ½–1 hour (depending on how crunchy or soft you like your soups), adding more stock (or water) if necessary.

Meanwhile, cook the pasta in plenty of salted boiling water, but remove from the heat and drain when only about half-cooked – well before the 'al dente' stage. Add to the soup just a few minutes before serving, and continue cooking until the pasta is as you like it. Season, and serve with plenty of freshly grated Parmesan on the side.

Basic Italian tomato sauce   ♡ ○

I love the Italian tomato sauces – they are not only the most
delicious of all (when prepared the right way), but also the
healthiest and least fattening as they contain no animal fat,
just a little olive oil. I have been working on the classical
Italian tomato sauce made with ingredients available in
England for some years now, and have to admit that the
following recipe is perfection, as well as being simple to make
(although it does have to simmer for quite a long time).
There are many optional variations in even this basic recipe.
Tastes are individual – I like to include lots of chilli and garlic
because I like spicy food, although in these recipes I have
included just enough of these to make the dishes 'perky'
without being too spicy. Feel free to adjust quantities or leave
out ingredients altogether according to your taste.
Wine depends on availability. I would think twice about
opening a bottle especially! As for herbs, I love oregano in
tomato sauces but you might prefer to use dried thyme or
sage, or fresh herbs from your garden. As fresh Italian plum
tomatoes are generally unavailable in Great Britain, I strongly
recommend using the tinned variety rather than English
tomatoes.
As you will see from the following pages, this recipe can be
used as a basis for many sauces. I would suggest making a
large quantity – perhaps double the amounts given here – and
then freezing it in cup-size portions, so that you can run up a
host of delicious pasta concoctions at a moment's notice.

**For 4 main course or 6–8 starter helpings (or 4 cupfuls for
freezing), use:**

> 2 tablespoons (2 × 15 ml spoons) good olive oil
> 1 large onion (6 oz/175 g), finely sliced
> 1 small dried red chilli (½ inch/1 cm) to taste (optional)
> 2–4 cloves garlic, crushed
> 3 oz (75–100 g) carrot, coarsely grated
> 1 very large tin (1 lb 12 oz/800 g) Italian plum tomatoes
> 2 tablespoons (2 × 15 ml spoons) tomato purée

2 bay leaves
2 teaspoons (2 × 5 ml spoons) dried oregano
½ glass white wine (optional)
1 teaspoon (1 × 5 ml spoon) sugar, caster or granulated
salt and pepper
12 oz (325–350 g) quills, or any other sort of pasta

Sauté the onion in the olive oil with the chilli and half the garlic until the onion is translucent and softened. Add the carrots and sauté for a further couple of minutes. Add the tin of tomatoes, breaking up the fruit with a wooden spoon. Add the tomato purée, bay leaves, oregano, wine, sugar and seasoning, stir well, then turn the heat up high. As soon as the sauce begins to bubble, stir it again and turn the heat down very low. Simmer for an hour, stirring occasionally and taking care not to let the sauce stick to the bottom of the pan or it will burn. Add the rest of the garlic about 10 minutes before the end of cooking. In a liquidizer or food processor, blend about three-quarters of the sauce until smooth. Mix together with the remaining quarter. Reheat gently just before adding to the pasta.

Meanwhile,* cook the pasta in plenty of salted boiling water until 'al dente'. Drain, and put back into the pan, or into a preheated serving dish. Add the sauce, stir together well, and serve immediately with cheese on the side (if you feel you need it).

* If you like your sauces really spicy, then before you add the sauce, toss the pasta in 2 or 3 tablespoons (2–3 × 15 ml spoons) olive oil into which you have crumbled some dried red chilli and a couple of cloves or crushed garlic. This also makes the dish more authentically Italian – they tend to use much more oil than the British.

Quills with tofu, roast red pepper and tomato sauce ♡ ○

Excellent for serving to vegetarians and vegans. Tofu (or bean curd) is one of the ideal foods – low in calories and cholesterols and high in protein. Some people find the flavour a little bland, but I like it and think it has a particularly pleasing texture. You could make a simpler version of this recipe by leaving out the roast red pepper, or substituting a couple of spoons of pine kernels if you have some.

If you like your sauces particularly spicy, then before adding to the sauce, toss the pasta in a spoon of oil to which you have added a crushed clove of garlic and half a finely chopped red chilli (or a very small one).

For 2 main course helpings, use:

> 1 red pepper
> 6 oz (175 g) firm tofu, cut into brick-shaped cubes
> 1–2 tablespoon (1–2 × 15 ml spoon) sesame seed oil, or
>   substitute a nut or vegetable oil
> Basic tomato sauce (see page 39), ¼ quantity
> 1 tablespoon (1 × 15 ml spoon) balsamic vinegar (optional)
> 6 oz (175 g) quills, plain or wholewheat

Place the whole pepper under a hot grill, with the flesh almost touching the heating element, and grill on all sides until the pepper turns completely black. Allow to cool and then peel off the black burnt skin. Deseed and cut the slightly cooked and softened pepper into strips and lay out on a plate. Dribble a spoon or so of oil over the strips, and leave for 10 minutes. Chop into smaller pieces.

Mix the balsamic vinegar (if using) together with the tomato sauce. At the last moment, sauté the tofu in the sesame seed oil until lightly browned, then add the red pepper and heat through. Heat the tomato sauce separately.

41

Meanwhile, cook the pasta in plenty of salted boiling water until 'al dente', drain, and put back into the pan. Toss together with the tomato sauce over a low flame, and serve out on to preheated plates in individual portions. Divide the tofu and red pepper evenly between the servings, spreading it on top. Serve immediately.

Spaghettini with roast red pepper, sun-dried tomatoes, butter beans and tomato sauce
♡ ○

The idea of spooning the tomato sauce on separately came to me after watching a Thai cook prepare a soup. Instead of heating all the ingredients together in the stock, she heated the noodles, bean sprouts, watercress and pork in hot water in a strainer, one portion at a time. She then laid the ingredients separately in the bottom of a soup bowl and poured over the stock. The whole operation, although time-consuming, was so pleasingly delicate that the idea of throwing everything together in a chaotic jumble seemed suddenly rather crude. This dish, with its characteristic but subtle flavours, seemed particularly appropriate to this approach.

For 2 light lunch or 3 starter helpings, use:

1 large red pepper
1½ tablespoons (1½ × 15 ml spoons) olive oil, and a little extra oil
1 clove garlic, crushed (optional)
3–4 sun-dried tomatoes, chopped
6 oz (175 g) tinned butter beans
4 tablespoons (4 × 15 ml spoons) Basic tomato sauce (see page 39) – about ½ cup or ⅛ basic recipe
6 oz (175 g) spaghettini or spaghetti

Place the whole red pepper on the grill pan, with the flesh almost touching the heating element, and grill on a high heat on all sides until the pepper turns completely black. Allow to cool and then peel off the black burnt skin. Deseed and cut the slightly softened pepper into strips and lay out on a plate. Dribble a spoon or so of oil over the strips, and leave for 10 minutes.

Meanwhile, cook the pasta in plenty of salted boiling water until 'al dente', drain, and return to the pan with the oil, garlic (if using), butter beans and sun-dried tomatoes. Toss over a low flame until well heated through. Arrange the pasta in portions on preheated plates. Spoon the reheated tomato sauce on to the middle of each serving. Serve immediately, with grated cheese only for those who feel they need it.

Spaghetti with puréed roast red pepper, chilli and tomato

♡ ○

This recipe was given to me by a very good friend, Rosamund Freeman Attwood, who leads an extremely hectic life as an actress, author, wife and mother. She adapted the ingredients from a Tunisian recipe. Ros and her husband give dinner parties at least twice a week to hordes of marauding fellow actors and other friends. She is an enthusiast of my first book, *Pastability*, and swears by pasta because it is quick and easy to prepare and always enormously popular.

For 4 main course or 6 starter helpings, use:

> 2 or 3 red peppers (approx. 1 lb/450 g)
> 12 oz (325–350 g) tomatoes, peeled and coarsely chopped
> 2–4 cloves garlic, crushed
> 3 tablespoons (3 × 15 ml spoons) olive oil
> ½ teaspoon (½ × 5 ml spoon) chilli powder (to taste)
> salt and ground black pepper
> 12 oz (325–350 g) spaghetti or quills
> 12–15 black olives, pitted and coarsely chopped
> 2 hard-boiled eggs, finely chopped or mashed with a fork,
> *or* (♡ omit boiled eggs) 4–6 oz (100–175 g) green beans or
>   mange-tout (snow peas)

Place the whole peppers on the grill pan, with the flesh almost touching the heating element, and grill on a high heat on all sides until the peppers turn completely black. Allow to cool and peel off the black burnt skin.* Cut into halves, remove the stalk and seeds, slice the softened pepper into strips and lay out on a plate. Dribble a spoon or so of the oil over the strips, and leave for 10 minutes or while you prepare the rest of the ingredients. Skin the tomatoes by putting them in a pan of lightly boiling water for a minute or so (the water in which you are about to boil the pasta will do just fine). Scoop them out with a slotted spoon, peel them and chop coarsely. Put the

---

* A useful tip is to put the hot, scorched red peppers into a covered dish or plastic bag and leave until cool. This will make the skin easier to peel off.

peppers, tomatoes, garlic, chilli powder and some salt and freshly ground black pepper in a liquidizer or food processor and blend. You should find that you have a sauce with the consistency and colour of tinned tomato soup.

Steam or lightly boil the green beans or mange-tout (if using) for just a couple of minutes until just cooked but still crunchy and green. Cut into 1 inch (2 cm) pieces.

Meanwhile, cook the pasta in plenty of salted boiling water until 'al dente', drain, and return to the pan with the sauce. Toss the sauce and pasta in the pan until well heated through, then add the beans (if using). At the last moment before serving, sprinkle over the olives and egg.

Quills with spicy tomatoes and aubergine ♡ ○

The long list of ingredients makes this recipe look more complicated than it is. A good vegetarian dish for those who like their vegetables slightly exotic and spicy.

For 2 main course or 3–4 starter helpings, use:

2 tablespoons (2 × 15 ml spoons) vegetable or nut oil
3 oz (75–100 g) onion, finely chopped
2 cloves garlic, crushed
2 teaspoons (2 × 5 ml spoons) fresh root ginger, finely grated
½ teaspoon (½ × 5 ml spoon) ground coriander
¼ teaspoon (¼ × 5 ml spoon) chilli powder
1 large or two small aubergines (10–12 oz/275–350 g)
10 oz (275 g) tinned Italian plum tomatoes, chopped
2 teaspoons (2 × 5 ml spoons) tomato purée
2 tablespoons (2 × 15 ml spoons) white wine or stock
4 tablespoons (4 × 15 ml spoons) yoghurt
(♡ ○ low-fat yoghurt)
2 tablespoons (2 × 15 ml spoons) fresh coriander, finely chopped (optional)
7 oz (200 g) quills or shells

Wrap the aubergines in foil and cook in a medium to hot oven (400°F/200°C/gas mark 6) for 40 minutes. Cut them in half, scoop out the flesh and mash. Slice the skin into thin strips.

Sauté the onion in the oil until softened and translucent. Add the garlic, ginger, ground coriander and chilli powder and continue to sauté for a couple of minutes. Add the aubergine pulp and continue to cook over a medium flame for another 3 or 4 minutes. Add the chopped tomatoes, wine and tomato purée and simmer for another 7 or 8 minutes, stirring occasionally. At the last moment before adding to the pasta, carefully stir in the yoghurt.

Meanwhile, cook the pasta in plenty of salted boiling water until 'al dente', drain, and put back into the pan. Pour over the sauce and heat through carefully. At the last moment add the aubergine skins and the fresh coriander (if using). Serve immediately on preheated plates.

Tagliatelle with leeks and porcini mushrooms

A really delicious and rather exotic combination – the rich taste of the porcini blends particularly well with the cream and the egg pasta. Serve as a starter on any occasion, but be prepared for requests for second and third helpings.

For 2–3 main course or 4 starter helpings, use:

½ oz (15 g) dried porcini mushrooms
¾ oz (20 g) butter
6 oz (175 g) leeks, sliced
4 tablespoons (4 × 15 ml spoons) double or single cream
1 tablespoon (1 × 15 ml spoon) white wine or dry Martini
6 oz (175 g) tagliatelle

Put the porcini into a small bowl and cover with a wine glass of water. Leave to soak for 20–30 minutes. Sauté the sliced leeks in the butter until softened, cover, and stew in their own juices for the next 10 minutes over a low flame, stirring every so often and taking care not to let them burn.

Drain the mushrooms, reserving the liquid. Chop into smallish pieces, then add the mushrooms and their soaking liquid to the leeks and butter. Continue cooking for a few minutes until the liquid has reduced by about half. Stir in the cream and white wine. Heat through gently just before adding to the pasta.

Meanwhile, cook the pasta in plenty of salted boiling water until 'al dente', drain, and put into a preheated serving dish. Pour on the reheated sauce and mix together thoroughly. Serve immediately, and avoid cheese unless people demand it – it is better without.

Rigatoni with sesame seed oil, carrots, fresh coriander, pine kernels and spice ♡ ○

An unusual combination of the slightly sweet and the spicy – an art perfected in the Middle East but which the British often get so wrong. It looks good too, with the crisp orange of the carrot flecked with the green of the fresh coriander.

I happened to use rigatoni (large ribbed pasta tubes) when I made this recipe, but you could use bows, shells or quills. Avoid spaghetti or linguine – they demand an oily or creamy sauce that clings to the strands; this one would just slide off!

For 3 light main course or 4–5 starter helpings, use:

> 1 tablespoon (1 × 15 ml spoon) sesame seed oil
> 1 tablespoon (1 × 15 ml spoon) vegetable or nut oil
> 2–3 extra spoons of either type of oil
> 3 oz (75–100 g) onion, finely sliced
> 4 cardamom pods, crushed
> 1 clove garlic, crushed
> 1 teaspoon (1 × 5 ml spoon) fresh root ginger, finely chopped or grated
> ½ teaspoon (½ × 5 ml spoon) fenugreek seeds (optional)
> ¼ teaspoon (¼ × 5 ml spoon) ground coriander
> 12 oz (325–350 g) carrots, finely chopped
> juice of one large orange
> grated nutmeg
> 2 tablespoons (2 × 15 ml spoons) pine kernels
> 2 tablespoons (2 × 15 ml spoons) fresh green coriander, finely chopped
> 9 oz (250 g) rigatoni or bows

Sauté the onion, cardamom pods, garlic and ginger in the sesame seed oil combined with the vegetable oil over a low flame until the onion is translucent and well softened. Very finely chop the carrots and add, with the fenugreek seeds, ground coriander and an extra spoon of oil, to the mixture in the pan. (If you have a food processor, use it to chop the carrots with the fenugreek seeds.)

Sauté for a further couple of minutes, then add the orange juice. Cover and stew for about 10 minutes, or until the carrots are softened to your taste. Add a grating of nutmeg (to taste), the pine kernels and, at the last minute before adding to the pasta, the coriander. Season to taste.

Meanwhile, cook the pasta in plenty of salted boiling water until 'al dente', drain, and put into a preheated serving dish. Toss the pasta in 1 or 2 tablespoons (1–2 × 15 ml spoons) of the extra oil, then stir in the reheated sauce. Serve immediately – without cheese!

Baked tagliatelle with spinach, eggs and cheese

A very pleasant and economical supper or lunch dish – a lot easier than lasagne but with the added advantage of being baked, so it can be prepared in advance. If you can't find fresh spinach in the shops and don't want to use frozen, you could always substitute spring greens, sliced and then steamed or boiled.

I recommend using good-quality dried tagliatelle rather than the fresh product. As I said in the Introduction, most of the so-called 'fresh' pasta in Britain is made from the wrong sort of flour, is therefore less nutritious, and is liable to pass from the uncooked, flour dough stage directly to sticky, glutinous and over-cooked. For this recipe I would recommend the pasta all'uovo made by F.lli de Cecco di Filippo, but if this is not available I would use the also excellent brand Barilla.

For 4–6 main course helpings, use:

> 1 oz (25 g) butter
> 4 oz (100–125 g) onion, finely sliced
> 1–2 cloves garlic, crushed
> 1 lb (450 g) fresh spinach, *or* 8 oz (225 g) frozen spinach, chopped or leaf
> 4 fl oz (125 ml) cream
> grated nutmeg to taste
> rind of ½ lemon, grated
> 6 eggs
> 4 oz (100–125 g) chopped ham (optional)
> 8 oz (225 g) tagliatelle

For the béchamel sauce

> 1½ oz (35–40 g) butter
> 1½ oz (35–40 g) flour
> 1 pint milk
> 4 oz (100–125 g) Cheddar cheese, grated, or substitute ½ quantity Emmenthal or fresh Parmesan

Sauté the onion and garlic in the butter until softened and translucent. Carefully wash the spinach in lots of cold water. In a medium to large pan steam the spinach (covered) in a few tablespoons (15 ml spoon) water and milk (it will reduce in bulk quite considerably, so if at first all the spinach does not fit in the pan, don't worry – just keep adding more as it shrinks). If using frozen, cook according to the instructions on the packet. Strain, pressing the spinach against the colander or sieve to remove as much liquid as possible. Chop the spinach coarsely (if not already chopped), then add to the onion and garlic in the pan. Sauté for a further few minutes before adding the lemon rind and nutmeg (a few gratings to taste) and then the cream and seasoning.

Boil the eggs for 7–8 minutes (or 10 if they are straight from the fridge). Cool them in cold water, then remove the shells.

Make the béchamel sauce following the instructions on page 169. Stir in half the grated cheese.

Cook the tagliatelle in plenty of salted boiling water until 'al dente'. Drain, and put back into the pan with a spoonful of oil or butter and half the ham (if using). Toss together and leave while you prepare for the next stage. (If you have, as recommended, used good-quality dried pasta and cooked it until 'al dente' it will sit quite happily for as long as you like without sticking together.)

Using an ovenproof dish about the size of a large soufflé dish, spread the spinach mixture over the bottom and then lay the eggs (whole) on top at regular intervals. Spread the tagliatelle evenly over the eggs and spinach, pour over the béchamel sauce, and sprinkle over the remaining ham and cheese. Cover the dish with foil and bake in a preheated oven (375°F/190°C/gas mark 5) for 30 minutes (at least), removing the foil for the last 15 minutes to allow the dish to brown. If it still does not seem brown enough, place under a hot grill for a few minutes, and then serve immediately.

The Actors' Centre lentil and spinach lasagne

Actors are by nature gregarious and friendly creatures who like to be 'where the action is'. The Actors' Centre fulfils a very necessary function by providing us Thespians who don't like pubs with a place to go, where we can study plays and techniques, acquire new skills and talk to each other. The Centre has always made a point of providing delicious and healthy food at extremely reasonable prices.

This lasagne recipe was given to me a couple of years ago by their chef at that time, Elaine Fradley, and is surprisingly light and fresh. If you are not vegetarian you could indulge in a richer, heavier and absolutely scrumptious version by substituting the lentil sauce from Ribbed snails with lentils and bacon (page 101) for the more demure lentils with lemon juice and white wine in this recipe.

For 4 main course helpings, use:

> 8 oz (225 g) continental lentils
> 1 tablespoon (1 × 15 ml spoon) butter, and a further 2 oz
> (50 g) butter
> 1 large onion (6 oz/175 g), finely sliced or chopped
> 2 bay leaves
> 1½ pints (850 ml) water
> 2 cloves garlic, crushed
> 1 tablespoon (1 × 15 ml spoon) parsley, finely chopped,
> *or* 1 tablespoon (1 × 15 ml spoon) fresh coriander, finely
> chopped
> 4 tablespoons (4 × 15 ml spoons) white wine (optional)
> 4 tablespoons (4 × 15 ml spoons) lemon juice
> zest of one lemon, grated
> 1½ lb (675 g) spinach, fresh or frozen
> 1 lb (450 g) soft white cheese (curd, cottage, 'quark' or
> fromage frais)
> 2 eggs
> 3 oz (75–100 g) cheese, grated – strong Cheddar,
> Emmenthal or Gruyère

grated nutmeg
salt and pepper
8 oz (225 g) lasagne

Sauté half the sliced or chopped onion in the spoon of butter until translucent and softened. Add the lentils, bay leaves and water and simmer for 30–40 minutes, until the lentils are softened.

Wash the spinach (if using fresh). Whether using fresh or frozen, cook on a low flame with no extra water, just 1 oz (25 g) of butter, in a covered pan for 7 minutes (or until defrosted). Add the grated zest of lemon and 1 tablespoon of lemon juice. Season with nutmeg, salt and pepper to taste.

Sauté the garlic and the rest of the onion in 1 oz (25 g) of the butter. Add the lentils, parsley or coriander, wine and the remaining 3 tablespoons of lemon juice. Beat together the soft cheese and eggs and season.

Cook the lasagne as directed on page 4.

Grease a large, shallow ovenproof dish. Put in half the lentil mixture, half the spinach, one third of the egg and soft cheese mixture, and a light sprinkling of the grated cheese. Follow this with a layer of lasagne. Repeat the layers, ending with the remaining cheese mixture and a good sprinkling of grated cheese.

Bake in a preheated oven (400°F/200°C/gas mark 6) for about 45 minutes or until golden brown.

Aubergine, tomato and cheese lasagne

I have to admit that I find lasagne hard work. I am not a perfectly organized cook in a perfect kitchen, nor am I particularly patient, and indeed on one occasion I ended up with pots and pans everywhere, tomato sauce on the floor and walls (something to do with detaching the food processor too quickly) and burnt fingers from trying to handle the lasagne before I had rinsed it. But no matter, the lasagne itself was absolutely delicious!

The big advantage of lasagne (and all baked pastas) is that everything can be prepared beforehand, so that if you are making a dinner for friends, by the time they arrive the kitchen can be spotless and the dish itself happily bubbling away in the oven.

I have made this dish for my parents, uncle and aunt. Auntie Christine is a strict vegetarian, while my father basically believes that a meal isn't a meal if it doesn't include meat or fish. This lasagne fitted the bill perfectly – although meatless, it is substantial and special enough for any occasion, and spectacular, with its contrasting blacks, yellows and reds.

Serve with a luscious mixed green salad, if possible throwing in watercress, avocado, mushrooms, walnuts and anything else out of the ordinary. If you can't face juggling with the lasagne leaves, then make the dish substituting tagliatelle layered with the other ingredients in the same manner.

For 6–8 main course helpings, use:

> olive oil
> a little flour
> 1½ lb (675 g) aubergines
> 4 eggs, hard boiled
> 1 Italian Mozzarella cheese (5 oz/150 g), *or* substitute 4 oz (100–125 g) Gruyère, Emmenthal or mild Cheddar, or a combination, in each case thinly sliced

3 oz (75–100 g) freshly grated Gruyère or Emmenthal, or
Cheddar *and* –
1½ oz (40 g) freshly grated Parmesan, *or* extra of one of the
above cheeses
10–12 oz (275–325 g) lasagne, or wholewheat lasagne
sea salt and freshly ground black pepper

For the tomato sauce

2 tablespoons (2 × 15 ml spoons) olive oil
4 oz (100–125 g) onion, finely sliced
1 dried red chilli (about 1¼ inch/3 cm long), finely chopped
but including seeds
4 cloves garlic, crushed
4 oz (100–125 g) carrot, grated
1 lb 12 oz (800 g) tinned Italian plum tomatoes
3 tablespoons (3 × 15 ml spoons) tomato purée
2 teaspoons (2 × 5 ml spoons) sugar
1 small wine glass white wine (optional)
2 or 3 bay leaves
2 teaspoons (2 × 5 ml spoons) dried oregano

For the béchamel sauce

1 oz (25 g) butter
1 oz (25 g) flour
1 teaspoon (1 × 5 ml spoon) English mustard powder
1 pint (575 ml) milk
1 oz (25 g) onion
few peppercorns
2 or 3 bay leaves

Cut the aubergines into slices about ¼ inch (0.5 cm) thick. Lay
the slices on some kitchen roll or a clean tea towel, sprinkle
lightly with salt, and leave to sweat. After about 15 minutes
turn them over, and leave to sweat for another 15 minutes.
Lightly flour the pieces on both sides, and fry in olive oil.
Alternatively, arrange on generously oiled baking sheets,
dribble a little more oil on top of the slices and bake for about
half an hour in a hot oven (400°F/200°C/gas mark 6), turning
them over every seven minutes or so and adding more oil if
necessary. (Aubergines do tend to absorb a lot of oil, which is

not so good for the waistline or the bank balance but very good for the taste.) When cooked, put the aubergines aside until ready to layer into the lasagne.

Mash the hard-boiled eggs with a fork. Make a Basic tomato sauce, following the instructions on page 39, using two of the garlic cloves, crushed, at the beginning of the cooking and throwing in the other two, crushed, just before taking the sauce off the heat. Make a thin béchamel sauce following instructions on page 169 (version 1). Cook the lasagne as instructed on page 4.

Take a shallow ovenproof dish, no more than 3 or 4 inches (8 × 10 cm) deep and about 15 inches (38 cm) by 10 inches (25 cm) – I use an attractive oval earthenware dish which I can bring to the table. Spread a thin layer of the tomato sauce across the bottom, followed by a sprinkling of the egg and a couple of tablespoons of the béchamel, then a sprinkling of the grated cheeses. Now spread a double layer of the lasagne (or tagliatelle). Then start again with the filling ingredients, this time including a layer of the aubergine and the thinly sliced Mozzarella (these two ingredients are fairly rich, so the layer should not be too dense), and seasoning with a sprinkling of sea salt and black pepper. Follow by a double or even triple layer of lasagne. Carry on with these layers, as long as the ingredients last – ending with tomato sauce, béchamel, and a good sprinkling of the grated cheese.

Cover with foil so that the pasta will absorb some of the juices, and bake in a hot oven (400°F/200°C/gas mark 6) for 45–55 minutes, removing the foil for the last 10 or 15 minutes to allow the top to brown.

Fish and meat – quick and easy

Linguini with eggs, anchovies, olives, garlic and parsley

Another very easy dish, but with plenty of taste and 'bite'.

For 2 main course helpings, use:

> 2 eggs, hard boiled
> 4 tablespoons (4 × 15 ml spoons) olive oil
> 2–3 cloves garlic, crushed
> A little dried red chilli (to taste), crumbled into very small
>   pieces
> 5 anchovy fillets
> 2 tablespooons (2 × 15 ml spoons) parsley, finely chopped
> 6 oz (175 g) spaghetti
> sea salt and freshly ground black pepper
> 8–10 black olives, pitted and chopped

Soak the anchovies in a little milk for 10 minutes (this makes them slightly less salty) while you boil the eggs. Remove the anchovies from the milk, and chop quite finely.

Shell the eggs, then put them on a plate and mash with a fork. Measure the oil into a cup and add the crushed garlic, chilli, mashed eggs, chopped anchovies and parsley.

Meanwhile, cook the pasta in plenty of salted boiling water until 'al dente', drain, and return to the pan. Pour over the sauce and seasoning, and toss for a minute or so over a low flame. Sprinkle the chopped olives over the pasta, and serve immediately.

Spaghetti with olives, capers, anchovies, bacon and chilli

For 2 main course or 4 starter helpings, use:

2 tablespoons (2 × 15 ml spoons) extra virgin olive oil
4 anchovy fillets, coarsely chopped
½ inch (1 cm) dried chilli, chopped
2 tablespoons (2 × 15 ml spoons) capers, drained and
    chopped
8–10 black olives, pitted and cut into quarters
6 oz (175 g) spaghetti or fidelini ('sparrows' tongues', or
    thin linguini)
1–2 cloves garlic, crushed
4–5 rashers smoked streaky bacon
Tabasco sauce (optional)

In a medium-sized frying pan or saucepan, sauté the chopped anchovies and chilli in the oil until the anchovies have dissolved into a kind of paste. Stir in the capers and remove from the heat. Grill or fry the bacon until quite crispy, drain on a piece of kitchen roll and then cut into pieces (I find kitchen scissors quite handy for cutting bacon, whether cooked or raw).

Meanwhile, cook the pasta in plenty of salted boiling water until 'al dente', drain, and put into pan in which you have prepared the anchovy, chilli and caper paste. Throw in the olives, garlic and chopped bacon and heat over a low flame, turning the pasta continuously with a wooden spoon until well heated through and the sauce evenly distributed. Serve immediately on preheated plates with Tabasco, salt and freshly ground black pepper on the side. This dish does not really need any cheese, but if you insist, make sure it is fresh Parmesan cheese, grated medium or coarse.

Spaghettini with cherry tomatoes, chillies, anchovies, garlic and basil ♡ ○

If cherry tomatoes are not available, this recipe can be made with the same quantity of coarsely chopped ordinary tomatoes, but make sure they are ripe and *tasty*, not the wet-flannel, slush-pink apologies for the fruit sold nowadays in so many supermarkets and greengrocers.

For 2 diet portions use:

2 teaspoons (2 × 5 ml spoons) olive oil
¼ dried red chilli (to taste), finely chopped
2 anchovies
(♡ omit the anchovies)
1 clove garlic, crushed
6 oz (175 g) cherry tomatoes, sliced into halves
fresh basil leaves (if available)
salt and freshly grated black pepper
4 oz (100–125 g) spaghettini

Soak the anchovies in a little milk, drain on a kitchen towel, then chop coarsely. Sauté the anchovies and chilli in the olive oil and add the crushed garlic. Toss the tomatoes for a minute or so in the mixture over a medium heat. (This can best be done at the last moment before draining the pasta, so as to preserve the freshness and texture of the tomatoes.)

Meanwhile, cook the spaghettini in plenty of salted boiling water until 'al dente', drain, and put back into pan. Add the sauce, salt and pepper, and stir over a low heat for a couple more minutes until well mixed and heated through, adding the basil leaves at the last moment. Serve immediately with grated Parmesan cheese on the side (if you can afford the calories).

Twists with anchovies, chilli, garlic and walnuts

This recipe, although not particularly glamorous in appearance, is quite delicious yet quick and easy to prepare – an excellent storecupboard standby. Because this dish contains fish in the form of anchovies, traditionally it does not require grated cheese on the side.

It is hard to be precise about quantities of chilli and garlic, as this is really a question of taste. I like very spicy food with lots of garlic. After all, garlic is extremely good for you – if ever I feel a cold coming on I find a good dose of the stuff virtually raw is the perfect cure. But for those who are not so enthusiastic about its taste or beneficial properties, there is a solution. Instead of using the garlic crushed, use a whole clove or two in the sauce to flavour the oil and then remove just before adding to the pasta.

For 2 main course helpings, use:

> 3 tablespoons (3 × 15 ml spoons) good olive oil
> ¼ dried chilli (to taste), finely chopped (or substitute chilli powder or a dash of Tabasco sauce)
> 8 anchovies
> 1–2 large cloves garlic, crushed
> 12 walnut halves
> 6 oz (125 g) twists

Soak the anchovies in a little milk for 10 minutes or so. Pour off the milk, and chop the anchovies coarsely. Heat the chilli and anchovies in the oil, stirring occasionally with a wooden spoon, until the anchovies have dissolved. Add the garlic and walnuts and continue to cook gently for a couple of minutes, taking care not to let the oil get too hot or the garlic will burn and become bitter.

Meanwhile, cook the pasta in plenty of salted boiling water until 'al dente', drain, and put back into the pan. Pour on the sauce, mix together thoroughly over a low flame, then transfer to a preheated serving dish, or directly on to preheated plates. Serve immediately.

Linguini with anchovies, sun-dried tomatoes, black olives, parsley and lemon peel

A very simple but attractive dish with the red, black, yellow and green of the ingredients contrasting nicely with the glistening off-white of the pasta. As with all simple dishes, the important point is to use the best basic ingredients you can find. Try serving it with a green, or chicory and raw mushroom salad.

Sun-dried tomatoes can be found in delicatessens in jars of all shapes and sizes, and they weigh very little individually so it is hard to be precise about quantities. The ones I use are about the size of a bay leaf, and I use 3 or 4, weighing just under 1 oz (25 g) in all. If these delicious, slightly piquant delicacies are not available to you, then replace with roast red pepper (see page 41) – about half a pepper will be adequate.

For 2 light lunch helpings, use:

> 2 tablespoons (2 × 15 ml spoons) virgin olive oil
> ½ inch (1 cm) dried red chilli (to taste), finely chopped
> 4–5 anchovy fillets
> 1–2 cloves garlic (to taste), crushed
> 3 or 4 sun-dried tomatoes, sliced
> 8 black olives, pitted and chopped
> pared peel of ½ lemon, finely sliced
> 2 tablespoons (2 × 15 ml spoons) parsley, finely chopped,
>   *or* 2 teaspoons (2 × 5 ml spoons) dried oregano
> salt and freshly ground black pepper
> 5–6 oz (150–175 g) linguini or spaghetti

Soak the anchovies in a little milk for a few minutes, drain on a piece of kitchen roll, and chop coarsely. Sauté the anchovies and chilli in the oil in a medium-sized saucepan or frying pan until the anchovies have dissolved into a paste. Stir in the garlic and continue to cook gently for a half a minute, taking care not to let the garlic burn.

Meanwhile, cook the pasta in plenty of salted boiling water

until 'al dente', drain, and put back into the pan in which you have prepared the anchovy and garlic paste. Throw in the remaining ingredients – the sun-dried tomatoes, olives, lemon peel and parsley or oregano – and toss well over a low flame. Season with sea salt and freshly ground black pepper. Serve immediately on preheated plates. Cheese is not really necessary with this dish, but if you insist, make sure that it is fresh Parmesan, *coarsely* grated. If fresh Parmesan is not available, then substitute fresh Gruyère or farm Cheddar.

Quills or shells with avocado, lemon and prawns

Simple and quick to make, this is a good dish for a party – you can make it even prettier to look at and add an extra interesting taste with a roast red pepper, sliced into little strips (see page 41 for instructions on preparation), or about 4 oz (100–125 g) French beans, steamed or boiled for just a few minutes to retain their crispness and colour. This dish can be made without the prawns, especially if you are using a colourful vegetable.

For 3 main course or 6 starter helpings, use:

>1 ripe avocado
>3 tablespoons (3 × 15 ml spoons) lemon juice
>4 or 5 shakes of Tabasco sauce (to taste)
>1 teaspoon (1 × 5 ml spoon) grainy or Dijon mustard
>5 fl oz (150 ml) single or double cream
>1 clove garlic, crushed
>4–6 oz (100–175 g) prawns or shrimps, precooked
>9–12 oz (200–350 g) quills or shells
>sea salt and freshly ground black pepper

Peel the avocado and cut into quarters, leaving one quarter still attached to the stone (the stone helps to stop the avocado turning brown). Sprinkle this quarter with 1 tablespoon (1 × 15 ml spoon) lemon juice and put aside for garnish at the end, cutting into slices just before adding to the pasta. Cut the other three quarters into chunks and put on to a large plate with the crushed garlic. Mash with a fork. Put the remaining lemon juice into a cup, add the spoon of mustard and mix together well. Mash the lemon juice and mustard together with the avocado and garlic and then the cream. Season with the sea salt and black pepper. (You could combine these ingredients in either a liquidizer or food processor, but I find it almost easier to mash them by hand, unless you are making a large quantity.) At the last moment, heat the sauce gently with the cooked prawns in a double boiler. (As I don't possess one,

I heat it in a small saucepan placed inside a larger one half full of water – as long as you make sure the water doesn't boil over into the sauce, this method works just fine!)

Meanwhile, cook the pasta in plenty of salted boiling water until 'al dente', drain, and put back into the pan or into a preheated serving dish. Mix together with the sauce, and serve immediately on preheated plates, with the sliced pieces of reserved avocado scattered across the top. Serve extra Tabasco rather than cheese on the side.

Tagliatelle with smoked salmon, capers and cream

This recipe was given to me by oil baron, diplomat and great host Baron Ricky di Portanova. Ricky and his wife Sandra live in great style between Acapulco, Houston and Claridge's in London, and dine in the finest restaurants in the world. However, every so often a longing for this particular dish seizes them, and Ricky orders the ingredients and a hot plate to be brought to the restaurant table, whereupon he prepares this delicious dish for his guests and himself.

An optional extra would be to garnish with chopped parsley or fresh coriander, or even salmon eggs.

For 2 main course or 4–5 starter helpings, use:

> 4 oz (100–125 g) smoked salmon, cut into pieces
> juice of ½ lemon
> sea salt and freshly ground black pepper
> 5 fl oz (150 ml) single or thin double cream (or half and
>   half of each)
> 1 generous tablespoon (1 × 15 ml spoon) butter
> 4 tablespoons (4 × 15 ml spoons) capers, drained
> nutmeg, grated, to taste
> 7 oz (200 g) egg tagliatelle (de Cecco, if you can find it)
> Swiss cheese (Emmenthal or Gruyère)

Cut up the salmon using a sharp knife or kitchen scissors. (The smell of fish can be removed by later rubbing the scissor or knife blades with the used half-lemon.) Put on a plate and squeeze over a light sprinkling of lemon juice and some black pepper.

Cook the pasta in plenty of salted boiling water until 'al dente', drain, and put back into the pan with the spoon of butter. Quickly heat the cream, watching it carefully and taking it off the flame just after it starts to boil. Add the capers. Toss the pasta with the butter until the butter has melted and coated the pasta. Pour on the capers and cream. Season with sea salt, a little more freshly ground black pepper and a little grated nutmeg, and toss again. At the last moment before serving, mix in the salmon pieces, retaining a few to sprinkle on the top. Serve with freshly grated Swiss cheese on the side.

Tagliatelle with avocado, anchovies and black olives and/or grilled bacon

This sauce has a pleasing smooth texture which goes well with the tagliatelle, coating it all over and tinting it pale green. It is important to have either the black olives or the bacon (or both) – they add that important touch of extra flavour and colour. This would make a good starter for a dinner party.

Buying olives can be a risky business; some varieties, although large and interesting to the eye, are completely tasteless. I would recommend using the smallish kalamata black olives, which are always tasty.

For 2 main course or 4 starter helpings, use:

> 1 large ripe avocado
> 5 anchovies
> 2–3 cloves garlic, crushed
> 3 tablespoons (3 × 15 ml spoons) olive oil
> 1 tablespoon (1 × 15 ml spoon) freshly squeezed lemon juice
> sea salt and freshly ground black pepper
> 10 black olives, pitted and chopped into halves or thirds
> *and/or* 3 oz (75–100 g) bacon, preferably thinly cut streaky, derinded
> 6 oz (175 g) tagliatelle

Peel the avocado and cut into quarters, leaving one quarter attached to the stone to prevent browning. Put aside this quarter for garnish, cutting into slices just before adding to the pasta. Cut the other three quarters into chunks, put on a plate with the anchovy fillets and crushed garlic, and mash with a fork. Incorporate the lemon juice and *two* spoons of the olive oil. Season with sea salt and black pepper.

If you are using the bacon, grill on both sides under a hot grill until as crispy as possible. Cut into bite-sized pieces (I find kitchen scissors very handy for this operation) and put on a piece of kitchen roll in the oven (on low) to keep warm.

Meanwhile, cook the tagliatelle in plenty of salted boiling water until 'al dente', drain, and put back into the pan with the remaining spoon of oil. Toss quickly over a low flame, add the sauce, and continue tossing the pasta in the sauce until the pasta is evenly coated. Put on to a preheated serving dish, or serve individually on preheated plates. At the last moment sprinkle over the olives or bacon and the sliced avocado pieces. Serve with chilli or Tabasco sauce on the side.

Linguini with tomatoes, anchovies, olives, capers and optional sun-dried tomatoes and pine kernels

This is really a luxurious and quick to cook version of the 'Putanesca' sauce inspired by one of my favourite restaurants in London, Orso in Covent Garden. Orso has the unfair advantage of seeming to be able to lay their hands on the most exquisite fresh ingredients, such as fresh Italian plum tomatoes, arugula lettuce and buffalo Mozzarella – ingredients denied to the ordinary mortal living outside Italy. To make up for the lack of the fresh plum tomatoes, I have added optional sun-dried tomatoes and pine kernels – optional because if you don't happen to have any in the larder, I wouldn't want to put you off making this absolutely delicious dish. This is one of my all-time favourites – spicy, healthy, easy to cook and attractive to look at – never fails to hit the spot! Believe it or not, it's also a storecupboard standby.

For 3 main course or 4–6 starter helpings, use:

   3 tablespoons (3 × 15 ml spoons) extra virgin olive oil
   3 oz (75–100 g) onion, finely chopped (red, if available)
   1 small dried red chilli, finely chopped (approx. 1¼ inches/
      3 cm long)
   5 anchovy fillets, coarsely chopped
   medium tin (14 oz/400 g) Italian plum tomatoes
   2½ tablespoons (2½ × 15 ml spoons) tomato purée
   2–3 cloves garlic, crushed
   4 large green and 4 large black olives, pitted and coarsely
      chopped (or use 8 of either colour)
   1 tablespoon (1 × 15 ml spoon) capers, drained
   4 sun-dried tomatoes, chopped (optional)
   2 tablespoons (2 × 15 ml spoons) pine kernels (optional)
   10 oz (275 g) linguini or spaghetti

Sauté the onion in the oil with the chilli and anchovy fillets until the onion is translucent and softened. Add the tinned tomatoes, breaking them up with a wooden spoon. Turn up the heat and continue to cook, stirring very frequently and taking care not to let it burn. After a few minutes add the purée, garlic, olives, capers and sun-dried tomatoes and simmer, covered, stirring frequently, for about another 10 minutes or until the sauce thickens into a loose purée consistency. Season to taste.

Meanwhile, cook the pasta in plenty of salted boiling water until 'al dente', drain, and put into the pan with the sauce. Toss the pasta and sauce together over a low flame until heated through and well integrated. Sprinkle over the pine kernels and serve piping hot on preheated plates, with *no* cheese on the side!

Spaghetti with anchovies and mushrooms

A favourite with my family, all the more popular because not only is it quite delicious, it is also quick, simple and economical to prepare.

If you have the time it is worth making the effort to find really good mushrooms. I used some lovely ones called 'champignons marrons' which I found at my local supermarket – they resemble a large and especially firm button mushroom, but are dark brown in colour. Another possibility would be to use large flat field mushrooms if available – they are particularly tasty.

For 2 main course or 4 starter helpings, use:

½ oz (15 g) butter, or 2 tablespoons (2 × 15 ml spoons) olive or nut oil
3 oz (75–100 g) onion, finely sliced
1–2 cloves garlic, crushed
4 anchovy fillets, coarsely chopped
6 oz (175 g) mushrooms, finely sliced
4 tablespoons (4 × 15 ml spoons) strong chicken stock (or substitute white wine, and a little extra oil or butter if necessary)
sea salt and freshly ground black pepper
6 oz (175 g) spaghetti

Sauté the onions in the oil or butter until translucent and softened. Add the garlic and the anchovies and sauté for another couple of minutes, stirring with a wooden spoon. Add the mushrooms and then simmer covered for a further few minutes, stirring frequently and adding the chicken stock after the first minute or so. Season to taste.

Meanwhile, cook the pasta in plenty of salted boiling water until 'al dente', drain, and put back into the pan. Pour over the sauce and heat through over a low flame, stirring continuously. Serve immediately, with cheese on the side only if your friends and relations clamour for it.

Quills with Italian sausage, chilli, tomato and oregano

For this recipe I use a precooked spicy Italian sausage from my local deli. The sausage is a variety of salami and apparently similar to the Spanish 'chirote' sausage. You could also use a 'Pepperoni' sausage. Whatever you decide to use, it should be precooked and spicy.

The balsamic vinegar in this recipe adds a particularly good tang to the taste. If you don't happen to have invested yet in a bottle of the stuff, don't be deterred! Either leave out the ingredient altogether, or else mix up your own concoction of similar taste, using rich red wine or port combined with an equal quantity of red wine vinegar.

Of course, the big problem in Britain is finding any tomatoes worth eating! If you cannot find any decent tomatoes, substitute some Basic tomato sauce (page 39), about one cupful or a quarter of the basic recipe.

For 2 main course helpings, use:

> 2 tablespoons (2 × 15 ml spoons) olive oil
> 4 oz (100–125 g) onion, finely sliced
> red chilli, fresh or dried, to taste
> 2 cloves garlic, crushed
> 4 oz (100–125 g) Italian hot sausage, sliced and slices cut into quarters
> 10 oz (275 g) fresh tomatoes, coarsely chopped (or substitute Basic tomato sauce, ¼ quantity)
> 1 teaspoon (1 × 5 ml spoon) oregano
> 1 tablespoon (1 × 15 ml spoon) balsamic vinegar, *or* substitute equal parts rich red wine or port and red wine vinegar
> 6 oz (175 g) quills

Sauté the onion in the oil with the chilli and garlic until the onion is translucent and softened. Add the chopped sausage and continue to cook over a low flame for a further 5 minutes or so. (If the sausage releases a lot of fat, pour it off at this point.) Add the tomatoes (or tomato sauce), oregano and balsamic vinegar (or wine mixture) and continue to cook for another few minutes, stirring frequently.

Meanwhile, cook the pasta in plenty of salted boiling water until 'al dente', drain, and put back into the pan with the sauce. Heat through again, and serve immediately on preheated plates.

More fish, chicken and meat

Chicken noodle soup

Probably one of my all-time favourite dishes. Soothing, delectable *and* not fattening. Last year we spent ten days in Hong Kong and every lunch-time we would fight our way past the ducks' gizzards and blackened webs, the snake soup and other unmentionables to seek out a bowl of chicken noodle soup. This is my version, which I freely admit is not a million miles from Granny's 'Jewish Penicillin'!

Good chicken stock is *very* useful in the cooking of pasta, especially Oriental dishes. It is an ideal way of providing a tasty liquid without too many calories. Chicken stock cubes are no real substitute, so whenever you find yourself with a chicken carcass on your hands, boil it up as follows. You can always store the stock in the deep freeze.

For 4 generous helpings, use:

For the chicken stock

> 1 chicken carcass
> 1 large carrot, coarsely chopped
> 1 medium onion, quartered
> 2–3 bay leaves
> a few peppercorns
> as available, a few outside leaves of a cabbage, lettuce,
>   leeks, etc., carefully washed
> about 3½ pints (2 litres) water

For the chicken noodle soup

> 1¾ pints (1 litre) chicken stock
> 2 oz (50 g) Chinese egg noodles, or substitute another thin
>   noodle (egg if possible) or spaghettini
> 8 oz (225 g) Chinese cabbage, spinach, lettuce, bean
>   sprouts, spring greens, or a combination of the above,
>   finely sliced
> 2 oz (50 g) mushrooms, finely sliced
> 3–4 oz (75–125 g) cooked chicken (leg or breast), sliced

Simmer the stock ingredients in the water for at least an hour, allowing to reduce by about a third but topping up with fresh

81

water if it reduces any more than that. Strain, and if it seems very oily, skim off the top layer of chicken fat. (The best way to do this is to cool the bowl of stock, refrigerate for several hours and then remove the hardened layer of yellow fat.)

For the chicken noodle soup, reheat the stock, add the vegetables and chicken and simmer for just a few minutes until the vegetables have softened. Meanwhile, cook the noodles separately in boiling water until also softened. Drain. Ladle the soup and vegetables into bowls, adding a small portion of the noodles to each serving. Serve immediately.

Carrot, watercress and pasta shell soup ♡ ○

This is a delicious soup, comforting without being too heavy. Contrary to the dull, murky appearance of so many soups, this one is an original bright orange!

For 4 helpings, use:

>   2 tablespoons (2 × 15 ml spoons) olive oil
>   4 oz (100–125 g) onion, finely sliced
>   1 clove garlic, crushed
>   1 bunch watercress, chopped
>   12 oz (325–350 g) carrots, finely chopped or coarsely
>   grated
>   2 pints (1.1 litres) chicken stock, preferably fresh
>   salt and freshly ground black pepper
>   8 oz (225 g) small pasta shells
>   freshly grated Parmesan, or another hard cheese
>   (♡ omit or go easy on the cheese!)

Sauté the onion and garlic in the oil over a low heat for several minutes, until the onion is translucent and softened. Stir in the chopped watercress, then the carrot and a little of the chicken stock, and cook for a further couple of minutes, stirring constantly. Add the rest of the stock and the seasoning, and simmer for about 15 minutes.

Meanwhile, cook the pasta in plenty of salted boiling water until about half done. Drain, and add to the soup. Continue to cook the pasta with the soup until the pasta is 'al dente'. Serve with grated Parmesan on the side.

Bows with smoked trout, leeks and cream ♡ ○

The colours of this dish are pale and pretty, so you may want
to serve a strongly coloured vegetable on the side – for
example steamed broccoli or a juicy mixed salad.
You may need to vary the amount of smoked trout,
depending on what is available. One whole medium smoked
trout will probably produce about 4–5 oz (100–150 g) of fillet.
You could also substitute 4 oz (100–125 g) smoked salmon,
thinly sliced and tossed together with the pasta and sauce just
before serving. Keep the Tabasco bottle handy for those people
who favour a little extra piquancy! And don't forget the lemon
juice; it really brings out the flavour of the smoked trout.

For 3 light main course or 4 starter helpings, use:

> 6 oz (175 g) smoked trout fillets, chopped into ½-inch
> (1–cm) pieces
> juice of ½ lemon
> salt and freshly ground black pepper
> 6 oz (175 g) leeks, sliced
> 4 tablespoons (4 × 15 ml spoons) double cream
> (♡ ○ substitute 4 tablespoons (4 × 15 ml spoons) low-fat
> yoghurt for the cream)
> pinch of nutmeg (finely grated), to taste
> 2 tablespoons (2 × 15 ml spoons) white wine or dry
> vermouth (or substitute extra cream)
> 8 oz (225 g) bows or butterflies

Squeeze some lemon juice over the chopped trout fillets,
followed by some freshly ground black pepper. Put to one
side. Steam or parboil the leeks until softened. Drain well,
then cook gently in the cream for a few minutes, adding the
wine and nutmeg half-way through. Add the smoked trout
and heat through well, just before adding to the cooked pasta.
   Meanwhile, cook the pasta in plenty of salted boiling water
until 'al dente', drain, and put back in the pan. Add the sauce
and heat gently over a low flame, mixing the pasta and sauce
continuously, until heated through and well integrated. Serve
immediately on well-heated plates with plenty of freshly
ground black pepper, but no cheese!

Spaghetti Machiavelli with king prawns, mushrooms, chilli, garlic and basil

Machiavelli is a restaurant in the heart of Sydney's business centre, decorated with villainous looking mug shots of some of Australia's more eminent politicos. To me, it is the ideal Italian trattoria: large, friendly, noisy, and serving heaped helpings of rustic fare which for abundance, flavour and freshness would shame most of its lackadaisical international counterparts. In the middle of the restaurant, Giovanni Toppi presides over a huge wooden table laden with antipasti: bowls of red peppers and Mozzarella, olives, omelettes, 20 kilo Parmesan cheeses, and a cornucopia of salad. Over this fantastic still-life is suspended a chandelier of whole prosciuttos, salamis and mortadellos. Shirt-sleeved lunchers can glance into the open-plan kitchen and observe Giovanni's daughter Paola nonchalantly tossing the 'specialità della casa' – an exquisite seafood pasta – in an enormous, spitting frying pan, while across the room her chicly attired sister writes the 'dockets'.

Paola explained that in Italy, where the butter is strangely white and tasteless, this dish would be made with oil, and she taught me a trick for preparing sauces which don't have much 'base'. She strains the pasta quickly and not too thoroughly, leaving in a little of the salted water in which the pasta was cooked. This adds just the necessary extra amount of liquid.

For 3 main course or 6 starter helpings, use:

> 6 tablespoons (6 × 15 ml spoons) butter
> 1 tablespoon (1 × 15 ml spoon) olive oil
> 3–4 cloves garlic, crushed
> 4 anchovies, chopped
> 1–2 small red chillies (fresh or dried) to taste, finely sliced
> sea salt and freshly ground black pepper
> 6 oz (175 g) mushrooms, finely sliced
> 30 fresh basil leaves, torn into halves – or substitute 2
>   tablespoons (2 × 15 ml spoons) fresh parsley or
>   coriander, finely chopped, or 1 dessertspoon (1 × 10 ml
>   spoon) oregano, dried

12 king prawns (cooked)
12 oz (325–350 g) spaghetti

Peel the king prawns and then split in half, deveining at the same time.

Cook the spaghetti in plenty of salted, boiling water until 'al dente'.

While the pasta is cooking, put all the remaining ingredients (except about a quarter of the fresh herbs) into a large frying pan, and sauté over a medium heat for about two minutes. Put aside until the pasta is ready.

Drain the pasta, allowing a little of the cooking water to remain, and put back into the pan. Meanwhile, gently reheat the seafood and mushroom sauce, add to the pasta, and then toss quickly over a medium heat until the pasta and sauce are well integrated and heated through. Put on to a preheated serving dish, or serve individually on to preheated plates. Sprinkle with the remaining fresh herbs and then serve immediately.

Wholewheat twists with ginger, crab and roast red pepper

An easy pasta dish made special by the use of sweet red peppers. Do not be tempted to substitute green peppers. Red may be more expensive but they're worth every penny, especially when prepared in this way. The slightly smoky flavour and softened texture of red peppers when roasted and peeled is quite different (and I think far tastier) than when they are prepared in the traditional ways. Tinned crab is also not exactly cheap, but by combining these two ingredients with pasta, I find a little goes a long way.

For 2 main course or 4 starter helpings, use:

> 3 tablespoons (3 × 15 ml spoons) good olive oil,
>   *or* 1 oz (25 g) butter
> 1 teaspoon (1 × 5 ml spoon) fresh root ginger, finely
>   chopped or grated
> 1 clove garlic, crushed
> salt and pepper
> 1 large or 2 small red peppers
> 1 tin (6 oz/175 g) crab meat in brine
> 4 fl oz (125 ml) single or double cream
> 7–8 oz (200–225 g) wholewheat (or plain) twists (or shells)

Place the whole red pepper(s) on the grill pan, with the flesh almost touching the element or flame. Grill under a high heat on all sides until the skin has turned black (watching carefully to make sure it doesn't actually catch fire!). When cool enough, peel off the burnt black skin, deseed and cut the softened pepper into strips. Lay out on a plate and sprinkle with olive oil (2 or 3 teaspoons) and a little salt and pepper. Leave for at least 10 minutes and then cut into smaller pieces.

Sauté the garlic and ginger gently in the butter or oil. Stir in the drained crab meat and the pepper, season and then pour over the cream, stirring carefully. Heat through gently and then put on one side until the pasta is ready.

Meanwhile, cook the pasta in plenty of salted boiling water

until 'al dente', drain, and put back into the pan. Pour over the sauce and cook together on a low heat for a couple of minutes, stirring continuously. Serve immediately on preheated plates and without Parmesan cheese. Parmesan should never be served with any pasta dish containing fish, and particularly this one – it would smother the delicate flavour.

Spaghetti with salmon, cream and tarragon

This really is one of my favourites, and very simple to make. I like the colours of this dish, and is easily good enough to serve as a starter at a dinner party.

Use fresh, not dried tarragon. I buy a cellophane packet from my local supermarket and use most of it, pulling the leaves away from the stalk and then chopping them coarsely.

For 2 main course or 4 starter helpings, use:

$\frac{3}{4}$ oz (20 g) butter
1 salmon steak (about 5 oz/150 g)
2 tablespoons (2 × 15 ml spoons) tarragon, chopped
4 fl oz (125 ml) double or single cream
3 tablespoons (3 × 15 ml spoons) white wine
6–8 oz (175–225 g) spaghetti

Remove the skin from the salmon, cut into six pieces, removing the biggest bone, and sauté with the chopped tarragon very gently in the butter for a few minutes in the bottom of a medium-sized frying pan. Take off the heat, transfer the salmon from the pan to a plate, and break into smaller-sized chunks, removing any remaining bones. Put back into the pan and pour over the wine and the cream. At the last moment, sauté again for a minute or so – *very* gently so as not to break up the salmon.

Meanwhile, cook the pasta in plenty of salted boiling water until 'al dente', drain, and return to the pan. Pour over the salmon and sauce, and serve immediately.

Quills with anchovies, grilled tomatoes and prawns

○

Serve this dish with a salad – cucumber and red pepper, or chicory, watercress and raw mushroom.

For 3 main course or 5–6 starter helpings, use:

> 12 oz (325–350 g) ripe tomatoes
> 2½ tablespoons (2½ × 15 ml spoons) olive oil
> sea salt
> 1 teaspoon (1 × 5 ml spoon) oregano
> 2 oz (50 g) onion, finely chopped
> 2 cloves garlic, crushed
> 4 anchovy fillets
> 4 oz (100–125 g) cooked shrimps or prawns, shelled
> 9 oz (250 g) quills

Cut the tomatoes in half and sprinkle with ½ tablespoon (½ × 15 ml) of the oil, some sea salt and the oregano. Grill until soft and well browned on top. Allow to cool and then scoop the flesh out of the skins with a spoon. Sauté the onion in the rest of the oil until translucent and softened. Soak the anchovies in a little milk for a few minutes, drain, and chop coarsely. Add the anchovies and the crushed garlic to the sautéd onion and continue to cook for a couple of minutes on a low flame. Add the grilled tomatoes and the prawns or shrimps, and cook gently for another 2 or 3 minutes. Season to taste.

Meanwhile, cook the pasta in plenty of salted boiling water until 'al dente', drain, and put back into the pan with the sauce. Heat through over a low flame, stirring continuously, until nice and hot and well mixed. Serve immediately without cheese on the side.

Spaghetti with tuna, capers and fromage frais

Fromage frais is available at most good supermarkets – I use 'Jockey' or 'Calin' (Yoplait) – but you could use Greek yoghurt instead. I like to use streaky, fine-cut (smoked Danish) bacon, because it grills so crisply.

For 2 main course helpings, use:

2 tablespoons (2 × 15 ml spoons) olive oil
4 oz (100–125 g) onion, finely sliced
7 oz (200 g) tin tuna fish, in brine or oil
½ wine glass white wine or chicken stock
4 oz (100–125 g) fromage frais or Greek yoghurt
2 oz (50 g) bacon
2 tablespoons (2 × 15 ml spoons) capers
6–7 oz (175–200 g) spaghetti

Open the tin of tuna fish, pour off the brine or oil and tip the fish on to a piece of kitchen roll to drain. Sauté the onion in half the olive oil until translucent and softened. Add the drained fish and continue to sauté for a couple of minutes, then add white wine and heat through. Season to taste. Take off the heat, cool and then liquidize with the fromage frais or yoghurt. Grill the bacon until well done and crispy, and chop or cut into 1-inch (2-cm) pieces.

Meanwhile, cook the pasta in plenty of salted boiling water until 'al dente', drain, and put back into the pan with the remaining tablespoon (15 ml spoon) of oil. Toss the pasta until evenly coated with the oil, pour over the tuna-fish sauce and heat over a low flame, stirring continuously, until heated through. Transfer to a preheated serving dish. At the last minute, throw on the capers and the bacon pieces.

Spaghettini with clams, bacon and optional spinach strips ○

The idea of using spinach is as much for the colour as anything else, as this dish is quite complete even without it. Very easy and quick to prepare. Serve with a green salad (including barely cooked green vegetables, e.g. beans or broccoli) and with chilled white wine, or even a glass of champagne.

For 3 main course or 4–6 starter helpings, use:

2½ tablespoons (2½ × 15 ml spoons) olive oil
2 cloves garlic, crushed
½ small dried red chilli, to taste, finely chopped
4 oz (100–125 g) onion, finely sliced
3 oz (75–100 g) smoked finely sliced bacon, chopped (○ omit bacon)
1 medium tin (10 oz/275 g) baby clams (including liquid)
scant ½ wine glass white wine or champagne
½ bay leaf or a pinch of powdered bay leaf
4 oz (100–125 g) fresh spinach leaves, washed and cut into thin strips (optional)
8 oz (225 g) spaghettini

Put the onion, chilli and 1 clove of crushed garlic with 1½ spoons of the oil into a small saucepan. Sauté for a couple of minutes until the onion is softened, then add the bacon and sauté until the bacon is browned. Add the wine, clam liquid and bay leaf, cover, and cook on a low heat until the liquid has reduced by about half. Put aside.

Meanwhile, cook the pasta in plenty of salted boiling water until 'al dente', drain, and put in a pan with the remaining spoon of oil and clove of crushed garlic. If necessary, keep warm until the sauce is ready.

Add the clams and the spinach strips (if using) to the onion and bacon mixture, and heat through *very* gently, stirring fairly frequently. (Too much heat too quickly will make the clams tough.) When just beginning to bubble around the edges, take off the heat and add to the spaghettini. Continue to heat through on a gentle flame until the dish is piping hot. Serve immediately with freshly ground black pepper, and Tabasco sauce (for those who indulge) on the side.

Linguini with tomato and seafood ♡ ○

An excellent strong and spicy seafood pasta, special enough to serve at a dinner party as either a starter or a main course. If you cannot find any one of the fish ingredients, substitute with something similar or increase the quantities of the other fish. Serve with a big mixed salad.

For 5–6 main course or 7–9 starter helpings, use:

> 3 tablespoons (3 × 15 ml spoons) olive oil
> 6 oz (175 g) onion (red, if available), finely sliced
> 4 cloves garlic, crushed
> 2 small dried red chillies, finely chopped (approx. 1¼ inches/3 cm long)
> 5 anchovy fillets
> (♡ omit anchovies)
> 6 oz (175 g) squid, ready cleaned and sliced
> 1 medium carrot (about 3 oz/75–100 g), grated
> 1 very large tin (1 lb 12 oz/800 g) Italian plum tomatoes
> 2 tablespoons (2 × 15 ml spoons) tomato purée
> ¾ wine glass red or white wine
> 1 teaspoon (1 × 5 ml spoon) dried thyme
> 1 oz (25 g) butter
> (♡ substitute a little olive oil for the butter)
> 6 oz (175 g) monkfish, or other firm white fish, cut into small chunks
> 4 oz (100–125 g) prawns, precooked and shelled
> 4 oz (100–125 g) mussels, precooked and shelled
> 4 oz (100–125 g) cockles, precooked and shelled
> 2 tablespoons (2 × 15 ml spoons) capers
> 6 black olives, pitted and chopped
> 15–18 oz (400–500 g) linguini, spaghetti or quills

Sauté the onion in the olive oil until translucent and softened. Add two of the cloves of crushed garlic, the chillies and the anchovy fillets, and sauté for another minute or so. Add the squid and sauté for a further couple of minutes, then add the carrot and sauté for another minute or two. Add the tin of tomatoes, breaking them up with a wooden spoon. Add the tomato purée, wine and thyme, and turn up the heat until the sauce bubbles. Give it a good stir, put the lid on, and simmer for about an hour on medium heat, stirring every so often and taking care not to let the ingredients burn or stick to the bottom of the pan. About ten minutes before the sauce has finished cooking, throw in the olives and drained capers.

Sauté the monkfish and the prawns in a separate pan with half the butter and a clove of crushed garlic until the monkfish is more or less cooked – opaque white. Put in the pan with the tomato and squid. Sauté the cockles and mussels for just half a minute or so with the remaining butter and clove of crushed garlic. At the last moment, add to the sauce and heat through.

Meanwhile, cook the pasta in plenty of salted boiling water until 'al dente'. Drain and put into a preheated serving dish. Mix in a couple of tablespoons of olive oil, and pour on the well-heated sauce. Mix together, and serve immediately on preheated plates.

Quills with chicken and tomato sauce ♡ ○

It is a well-known Italian trick to throw a piece of chicken into a tomato sauce to give it extra flavour – just a drumstick or two. In this version we throw in the whole chicken! There are several ways to serve this dish. You could serve the sauce with the pasta as a starter, then follow with the chicken pieces accompanied by a vegetable or salad. You could serve the two dishes at separate meals. Or you could serve the chicken pieces, pasta and sauce all together – or even make a lasagne. If possible, use a free-range or corn-fed chicken, and if you have one, cook this in a heavy iron casserole.

For 6 main course helpings, use:

3 tablespoons (3 × 15 ml spoons) olive oil
3 cloves garlic, crushed
1 small dried red chilli (approx. 1 inch/2 cm), chopped
   (optional)
8 oz (225 g) onion, finely chopped
1 chicken
1 medium carrot (2–3 oz/50–100 g), grated
1 medium stick of celery, finely chopped (optional)
1 very large tin (1 lb 12 oz/800 g) Italian plum tomatoes
2 tablespoons (2 × 15 ml spoons) tomato purée
1 wine glass red or white wine (optional)
1½ teaspoons (1½ × 5 ml spoons) dried oregano
2–3 bay leaves
salt and pepper
18 oz (500 g) quills or similar pasta shape

Joint the chicken into drumsticks, thighs and breasts, cutting each breast in half (reserving the remaining underpiece to boil up with an onion to make valuable chicken stock). Sauté the onion in the oil with the garlic and chilli. Lightly brown the chicken in the onion and oil, add the carrot and celery and sauté for a few minutes. Pour over the tinned tomatoes, breaking them up with a wooden spoon. Add the purée, wine and herbs, season to taste, then simmer for at least an hour, covered, on a low heat, stirring occasionally.*

Meanwhile, cook the pasta in plenty of salted boiling water until 'al dente'. Serve in one of the ways indicated in the opening paragraph.

* This chicken dish is even better when allowed to cool and reheated later, or even the following day.

Quills with lemon coriander chicken ♡ ○

A delicious, spicy and very attractive dish with its contrasting bright yellow and green. For this recipe I am indebted to *Sameen Rushdie's Indian Cookery*, an excellent book which I would heartily recommend to anyone at all interested in Indian cookery.

I have adapted the recipe for use with pasta, and cut down on the quantities of chilli and coriander. Ms Rushdie recommends the use of a wok rather than a saucepan to prepare the ingredients, as it helps to keep the chicken from breaking up too much.

For 3–4 main course helpings, use:

1 oz (25 g) butter
(♡ substitute oil for butter)
1 onion (4 oz/125 g), finely sliced
½ teaspoon (½ × 5 ml spoon) turmeric
3 cloves garlic, crushed
½ teaspoon (½ × 5 ml spoon) chilli powder
1 teaspoon (1 × 5 ml spoon) fresh root ginger, finely
   grated
2 chicken breasts (about 10 oz/275 g), bones and skin
   removed and cut into small slices or chunks
4 oz (100–125 g) plain yoghurt, thinned with a little water
(♡ low-fat yoghurt)
1 oz (25 g) fresh coriander, finely chopped, plus an extra
   2 tablespoons (2 × 15 ml spoons)
2 tablespoons (2 × 15 ml spoons) freshly squeezed lemon
   juice
½ wine glass white wine (optional)
1 tablespoon (1 × 15 ml spoon) olive oil
9 oz (250 g) quills or shells

Sauté the onion in the butter until translucent and well softened and beginning to turn golden brown. Add the turmeric, garlic, ginger and chilli powder and continue to stir fry on a medium heat, taking care not to let the spices burn. Put in the slices of chicken and continue to cook until the surfaces of the chicken slices change colour to an opaque yellow/gold. Thin the yoghurt, beating it together with a little water until it is the consistency of single cream, then pour it slowly into the pan, stirring all the time. Cover, and simmer over a low heat for 20–30 minutes, or until the chicken is very tender. A few minutes before the chicken is ready, pour in the lemon juice, white wine (if using) and 1 oz (25 g) of coriander.

Meanwhile, cook the pasta in plenty of salted boiling water until 'al dente'. Drain, and put on to a preheated serving dish with the sauce and the olive oil. Mix together well. Sprinkle the remaining coriander over the top and serve immediately.

Spaghetti with onions, olives and bacon

Use any bacon you like – smoked or unsmoked. If you have
some thinly cut streaky bacon, you could serve it crispy. Grill
the bacon until crisp, chop it up (or cut it with kitchen scissors)
and throw it on at the last minute. But if you do use the bacon
in this way, you will need to add an extra tablespoon (15 ml
spoon) of oil to the recipe below.

For 2 main course helpings, use:

> 3 tablespoons (3 × 15 ml spoons) olive oil
> 4 oz (100–125 g) onion, finely sliced
> 4 oz (100–125 g) bacon, derinded and chopped
> 8–10 black or green olives, pitted and chopped
> 6 oz (175 g) spaghetti
> fresh Parmesan cheese, or substitute Emmenthal or mild
>   Cheddar

Sauté the onion in the oil until translucent and softened. Add
the bacon and sauté until brown. Add the olives and sauté for
a further minute or two.

Meanwhile, cook the pasta in plenty of salted boiling water
until 'al dente'. Drain, and put back into the pan with the
sauce. Heat through, and serve immediately with the cheese
on the side.

Ribbed snails with lentils and bacon

This recipe was given to me by Arrelle von Hurter, who is one of those organized people who can cook a feast of highly original dishes for ten while dandling a couple of babies on her knee.

I used 'lumache rigate' – directly translated this means 'ribbed snails'. These are large pasta shapes which look a bit like snail shells, or even the U-bend section of a drainpipe! We would both recommend something fairly solid to balance out and 'catch' the lentils. Serve with a big mixed green salad into which you have put some lightly blanched green vegetables, for example sliced courgette, green beans, asparagus or raw spinach leaves.

For 3–4 main course helpings, use:

8 oz (225 g) green lentils
1 tablespoon (1 × 15 ml spoon) butter
1 large onion (6 oz/175 g), finely sliced or chopped
2 bay leaves
1½ pints (850 ml) water
1 oz (25 g) butter
2 cloves garlic, crushed
4 oz (100–125 g) thick-cut smoked bacon, finely sliced
2 tablespoons (2 × 15 ml spoons) white wine (optional)
4 fl oz (125 ml) single or double cream
8 oz (225 g) ribbed snails

Sauté half the onion in the spoon of butter until translucent and softened. Add the lentils, bay leaves and water and simmer for 30–40 minutes until the lentils are softened.

Sauté the remaining onion and the bacon with the crushed garlic in the ounce (25 g) of butter until the onion is translucent and softened and the bacon lightly browned. Add the cooked lentils, stir together, then add the wine (if using) and cream and stir together well.

Meanwhile, cook the pasta in plenty of salted boiling water until 'al dente'. Drain, and return to the pan with the lentil sauce. Transfer to a preheated serving dish and serve immediately.

Rigatoni with bacon, mushrooms and artichoke hearts

One of those dishes that really 'hit the spot'. I first experienced this exquisite combination of pasta, artichoke hearts and bacon in the town of Mackay on the Barrier Reef in Australia. It was served in a little Italian restaurant on the outskirts of the town, owned and run by a young Australian woman who had spent her student days in Florence. Her charming French boyfriend, Patrick, was the chef.

For 5–6 starter or 3–4 main course helpings, use:

½ oz (15 g) butter
4 oz (100–125 g) bacon (preferably smoked streaky), cut into small pieces
4 oz (100–125 g) onion, finely sliced
4 oz (100–125 g) mushrooms, sliced
14 oz (400 g) tin artichoke hearts (about 7), cut into quarters
5 tablespoons (5 × 15 ml spoons) strong chicken stock, or substitute half cream/half white wine
5 fl oz (150 ml) double or single cream
nutmeg, to taste (optional)
salt and pepper
10–12 oz (275–350 g) rigatoni or quills
Parmesan cheese, or substitute Gruyère or farm Cheddar

Sauté the bacon in the butter for a couple of minutes, add the onion, cover, and cook over a low heat, stirring occasionally, until the onion is well softened. Stir in the sliced mushrooms, and continue to cook covered for another few minutes. Add the artichoke hearts and cook for a further 3 or 4 minutes before adding the chicken stock and cream. (Use fresh chicken stock (see page 81), or else substitute extra cream and/or some white wine. Avoid chicken stock cubes – the taste is in no way comparable to the real thing.) Simmer very gently for another 3 or 4 minutes. Season, and grate in a little nutmeg. Gently reheat if necessary just before combining with the pasta.

Meanwhile, cook the pasta in plenty of salted boiling water until 'al dente', drain, and put back into the pan. Pour on the sauce, then gently cook the sauce and pasta together for a couple of minutes, stirring continuously, to allow the pasta to absorb some of the sauce. Serve with plenty of fresh coarsely grated Parmesan cheese on the side.

Shells with crispy bacon, mushrooms, mustard and Gruyère cheese

A pleasantly warming dish. Good for an autumnal evening. I like to use smoked rindless thin-cut streaky bacon – I find it grills particularly well and the result is both crispy and light. You could sprinkle some basil leaves, or chopped parsley or coriander, over this dish to provide some colour. Serve with a mixed green salad that includes watercress and/or raw spinach. If you can get hold of it, the most delicious green leaf of all is rocket, also known as arugula, which is well worth growing if you have a garden.

For 2 main course helpings, use:

> 2 oz (50 g) streaky smoked bacon (rindless or derinded)
> 1 tablespoon (1 × 15 ml spoon) butter
> 4 oz (100–125 g) onion, finely sliced
> 2 teaspoons (2 × 5 ml spoons) Dijon or other mild mustard
> 4 tablespoons (4 × 15 ml spoons) or ½ wine glass white wine
> 4 oz (100–125 g) mushrooms, finely sliced
> 4 fl oz (125 ml) single cream
> salt and pepper
> 6 oz (175 g) pasta shells
> 2 oz (50 g) Gruyère cheese, grated (*or* substitute Emmenthal, Jarlsberg or strong Cheddar)

Sauté the onions in the butter over a low flame until softened and translucent. Stir in the mustard and white wine, then the mushrooms. Continue to cook slowly over a low flame, stirring occasionally, for another few minutes, stir in the cream and simmer for just a couple of minutes more. Season to taste, remembering that the bacon will bring quite a salty taste to the dish when finished. At the last moment, while the pasta is cooking, grill the bacon until crispy but not burnt, put to drain on a piece of kitchen roll and, if necessary, keep warm.

Meanwhile, cook the pasta in plenty of salted boiling water until 'al dente', drain, and put back into the pan. Mix in the sauce and grated cheese, and heat through over a low flame, stirring frequently with a wooden spoon. Chop or cut (using kitchen scissors) the bacon into pieces. Serve up on a preheated dish, sprinkling the chopped crispy bacon over the top.

Spaghetti with veal and pork meatballs and tomato sauce

For 4–5 main course helpings, use:

For the meatballs

    2 slices (2 oz/50 g) white bread, toasted
    8 oz (225 g) pork, ground
    8 oz (225 g) veal, ground
    2–3 cloves garlic, crushed
    4 pinches chilli powder (to taste)
    nutmeg, two or three gratings (to taste)
    salt and pepper
    1 tablespoon (1 × 15 ml spoon) dried oregano
    2 eggs
    2 tablespoons (2 × 15 ml spoons) Parmesan cheese (*or*
       substitute Emmenthal or Cheddar), finely grated
    a little olive oil for frying

For the sauce

    Basic tomato sauce (page 39), ½ quantity
    ½ wine glass white wine, or substitute chicken stock or
       water

    12 oz (325–350 g) spaghetti
    1 tablespoon (1 × 15 ml spoon) olive oil

If you have a food processor, process the toast into
breadcrumbs then add the ground meat, herbs, chilli, garlic,
eggs, seasoning and Parmesan and process again. If you do
not have a processor, chop the toast as finely as you can, add
the nutmeg, oregano, chilli, a little seasoning and Parmesan
and mix together. Add the meat and mix well, then add the
eggs, which you have first beaten with a fork.

    Using the palms of your hands, roll the meat mixture into
little balls (about the size of small Brussels sprouts).

    Fry the meatballs in a little olive oil until browned all over. If you like garlic, add a crushed clove or two to the oil first.

At the last moment, take *half* the tomato sauce and put it with the wine into a pan big enough to hold the meatballs. Heat gently until well warmed, then add the meatballs. Continue cooking for a few moments to give the meatballs time to heat through and become flavoured by the tomato sauce.

Meanwhile, cook the pasta in plenty of salted boiling water until 'al dente', drain, and return to the pan over a low flame. Toss in the tablespoon of olive oil, then the remaining half of the tomato sauce. Serve immediately, either mixing in the meatballs and sauce or serving them separately. Serve grated cheese on the side if you feel the need.

Spaghetti with coriander and ginger meatballs and spicy tomato sauce

These meatballs are reminiscent of something you might eat in a very good Thai restaurant. Very flavoursome without being *too* spicy or exotic.

For 2 main course helpings, use:

For the meatballs

> 1 slice white bread, toasted
> 4 oz (100–125 g) veal, ground
> 4 oz (100–125 g) pork, ground
> 2 cloves garlic, crushed
> 2 decent pinches chilli powder (to taste)
> 1 teaspoon (1 × 5 ml spoon) dried oregano
> 1½ tablespoons (1½ × 15 ml spoons) fresh coriander, chopped
> salt and pepper
> 1 tablespoon (1 × 15 ml spoon) fresh root ginger, finely grated
> 1 egg
> 1 tablespoon (1 × 15 ml spoon) Parmesan cheese, grated
> a little vegetable or nut oil for frying

For the sauce

> Basic tomato sauce (page 39), ¼ quantity
> ¼ wine glass white wine, stock or water
> 1 tablespoon (1 × 15 ml spoon) fresh coriander, finely chopped

> 6 oz (175 g) spaghetti
> 1 tablespoon (1 × 15 ml spoon) oil
> pinch chilli powder
> 1 clove garlic, crushed

If you have a food processor, process the toast into breadcrumbs then add the ground meat, herbs, chilli, garlic, egg, ginger, seasoning and Parmesan and process again. If you do not have a processor, chop the toast as finely as you can, add the garlic, oregano, chilli, a little seasoning and Parmesan and mix together. Add the meat and mix well. Add the grated ginger and coriander to the egg and beat with a fork, then mix in with the meat.

Using the palms of your hands, roll the meat mixture into little balls (about the size of small Brussels sprouts).

Fry the meatballs in a little oil until browned all over. If you like garlic, add another crushed clove or two to the oil first.

At the last moment, take *half* the Basic tomato sauce and put it with the wine, stock or water into a pan big enough to hold the meatballs. Heat gently until well warmed, then add the meatballs. Continue cooking for a few moments to give the meatballs time to heat through and become flavoured by the tomato sauce. Add the chopped coriander.

Meanwhile, cook the pasta in plenty of salted boiling water until 'al dente', drain, and return to the pan over a low flame. Toss the pasta in the crushed garlic, chilli powder and extra tablespoon oil, then add the remaining half of the tomato sauce. Serve immediately, either mixing in the meatballs and their sauce or serving separately.

Bows with lamb kidneys, mushrooms, parsley and garlic

I've always found 'escargots' as served in French restaurants a rather overrated dish. The delicious part is without question the sauce – crushed garlic, parsley and pure melted butter, and lots of it! However, the automatic calorie and cholesterol counter in my brain prevents me from including anywhere in this book butter and oil in such quantities. If you think you can allow yourself the extra cholesterol and calories (100 calories per tablespoon/15 ml spoon of butter, oil or margarine), then feel free to increase my quantities of those ingredients.

Serve with a mixed green salad into which you have put some very lightly boiled or steamed green vegetables – for example green beans cut into 2-inch (5-cm) pieces, finely sliced courgettes, or broccoli cut into little florets, or a combination of the above. Make a dressing out of balsamic vinegar (or substitute red wine vinegar), oil and some grainy mustard.

For 2 main course helpings, use:

2 tablespoons (2 × 15 ml spoons) butter or olive oil
2 cloves garlic, crushed
2 tablespoons (2 × 15 ml spoons) parsley, finely chopped
6 oz (175 g) lamb kidneys (about 3)
4 oz (100–125 g) mushrooms, sliced
4–6 tablespoons (4–6 × 15 ml spoons) strong fresh chicken stock, white wine or water
1 additional tablespoon (1 × 15 ml spoon) olive oil
1 additional clove of garlic, crushed
1 additional tablespoon (1 × 15 ml spoon) parsley, chopped
salt and pepper
6 oz (175 g) bows or butterflies

Prepare the kidneys by removing any outer encasing membrane and cutting out and discarding the tough central sinew (kitchen scissors are good for this), then slice thinly.

Sauté the kidneys – in 1 tablespoon (1 × 15 ml spoon) oil or butter with 2 cloves of crushed garlic and 2 tablespoons (2 × 15 ml spoons) of chopped parsley – for 2 or 3 minutes, depending on how well done you like your kidneys (but bearing in mind that they go hard and rubbery if overcooked). Remove the kidneys, leaving as much of the butter or oil and juices as possible in the pan, and put aside. Put another tablespoon (15 ml spoon) of butter or oil in the pan and add the mushrooms. Sauté for a minute or two, then add the liquid (chicken stock, white wine or water), cover, and cook for a further few minutes. At the last moment before mixing with the pasta, add the kidneys, reheat, and season to taste.

Meanwhile, cook the pasta in plenty of salted boiling water until 'al dente', drain, and put back into the pan. Immediately add the additional oil, garlic and parsley, and mix together well. Put on a low flame and add the mushrooms, kidneys and sauce and mix together again until well integrated and heated through. Serve immediately on preheated plates, with plenty of freshly ground black pepper.

Rigatoni with meat, aubergine and spices

A strong, spicy meat sauce with an Indian influence – excellent fodder for Guy Fawkes' night! The fresh coriander is optional, as some people find it an acquired taste.

For 3 main course or 4–5 starter helpings, use:

> 3½ tablespoons (3½ × 15 ml spoons) olive or vegetable oil
> 8 oz (225 g) onion, finely sliced
> 3 cloves garlic, crushed
> 1 teaspoon (1 × 5 ml spoon) fresh root ginger, very finely
>   chopped or grated
> 1 small dried red chilli, finely chopped
> ½ teaspoon (½ × 5 ml spoon) turmeric
> 1 scant teaspoon (1 × 5 ml spoon) ground coriander
> a little nutmeg, grated
> 8 oz (225 g) minced beef
> 14 oz (400 g) tin Italian plum tomatoes
> 1 teaspoon (1 × 5 ml spoon) tomato purée
> 1 large aubergine (approx. 8–10 oz/225–275 g)
> 10 oz (275 g) rigatoni (large pasta tubes)
> 3 tablespoons (3 × 15 ml spoons) fresh coriander, finely
>   chopped (optional)

Wrap the aubergine in foil and cook in a medium to hot oven (400°F/200°C/gas mark 6) for 40 minutes.

Sauté half the onion in 2 tablespoons (2 × 15 ml spoons) of the oil until translucent and softened. Add the crushed garlic, chilli, ginger, turmeric and ground coriander and continue to sauté over a low flame, stirring continuously, for a couple of minutes, taking care not to let the mixture burn. Add the minced beef and two or three gratings of nutmeg and continue to cook, stirring frequently with a wooden spoon, until the beef is browned.

Separate the tomatoes from their juice and break them up either with a wooden spoon or by squeezing them through your fingers. Add the tomatoes, about half the juice, and the tomato purée to the meat, and simmer for about 20–25 minutes, stirring occasionally and taking care not to let the sauce stick to the bottom of the pan and burn, adding more of the tomato juice if and when necessary.

Sauté the rest of the onion in the remaining 1½ tablespoons (1½ × 15 ml spoons) oil until translucent and softened. Peel the skin from the aubergine while still warm, chop the aubergine, then add to the softened onion. Continue to cook over a low heat for 5–7 minutes, then add to the meat sauce. Simmer the mixture over a low heat for about 10 minutes, adding the rest of the tomato juice a little at a time each time you stir. Season.

Meanwhile, cook the pasta in plenty of salted boiling water until 'al dente'. Drain, and mix together with the sauce and the chopped fresh coriander (if using) in a preheated serving dish. Serve immediately on preheated plates, with fresh Parmesan cheese medium grated on the side.

Spaghetti with meat and tomato sauce

The tastiest of bolognese sauces! Quick to prepare if you've already made the tomato sauce.

For 2 main course helpings, use:

Basic tomato sauce (page 39), ¼ quantity freshly made or defrosted if made earlier and frozen
2 tablespoons (2 × 15 ml spoons) olive oil
3 oz (75–100 g) onion, finely sliced or chopped
1–2 cloves garlic, crushed (optional)
1 small dried red chilli (½ in/1 cm), finely chopped
1½ oz (40 g) bacon, derinded and chopped
8 oz (225 g) best minced beef (lean)
2 tablespoons (2 × 15 ml spoons) white wine (optional)
⅛ teaspoon (⅛ × 5 ml spoon) ground coriander
½ cup chicken stock, fresh or made with a pinch of chicken stock cube and hot water
8 oz (225 g) spaghetti or rigatoni (ribbed pasta tubes)
sea salt and black pepper
fresh Parmesan cheese, medium grated

Sauté the onion with the garlic and chilli in half the oil until the onion is translucent and softened. Add the bacon and continue to cook until the bacon has changed colour. Add the minced beef and cook until the mince has browned. Stir in the white wine (if using) and ground coriander, then pour in the chicken stock. Simmer for half an hour, taking care not to let the liquid boil away completely (adding more chicken stock or water if necessary). Stir in the tomato sauce and season.

Meanwhile, cook the pasta in plenty of salted boiling water until 'al dente', drain, and put back into the pan. Toss in a tablespoon of olive oil, then mix in half the sauce. Serve the pasta and sauce in portions on preheated plates, adding an extra dollop of sauce per person on the top. Serve immediately with sea salt, black pepper and grated cheese on the side.

Oriental – quick and easy

Linguini with soy sauce, ginger and garlic

Strongly influenced by Japanese cuisine. You could make this dish using buckwheat noodles, or 'soba noodles' as they are called in Japan. One of the joys of Japanese food is the use of soy sauce and although it is an acquired taste, once acquired it is positively addictive! There are a lot of rather dubious soy sauces on the market, made of all sorts of strange ingredients, which give the product a bad name, so do go out of your way to find one that is naturally brewed and pure. I would recommend the Japanese make Kikkoman, available in large supermarkets.

For an authentic touch, sprinkle on a little dried bonito fish shavings just before serving. These can be bought in little cellophane packets in any shop supplying Japanese ingredients. Don't be deceived by the unassuming appearance of this delicacy – the taste is subtle and exquisite.

As with so many Japanese flavours, a little goes a long way – so serve this dish as a starter.

For 4 starter helpings, use:

> 2 tablespoons (2 × 15 ml spoons) vegetable or nut oil
> 2 teaspoons (2 × 5 ml spoons) fresh root ginger, finely grated or chopped
> 1–2 cloves garlic (to taste), crushed
> ¼ dried red chilli (to taste), finely chopped
> 2 spring onions, finely sliced (optional)
> 4 tablespoons (4 × 15 ml spoons) soy sauce (Kikkoman)
> 3 tablespoons (3 × 15 ml spoons) white wine or apple juice
> 1 teaspoon (1 × 5 ml spoon) caster sugar
> 6–8 oz (175–225 g) linguini or spaghetti
> dried bonito fish shavings (optional)

Sauté the fresh ginger, garlic, chilli and spring onion in the oil for just a couple of minutes on a low flame, taking care not to let the garlic burn. Add the soy sauce, wine or apple juice and caster sugar and stir together.

Meanwhile, cook the pasta in plenty of salted boiling water until 'al dente', drain, and put back into the pan with the sauce. Heat through for a couple of minutes, stirring continuously with a wooden spoon. Serve immediately on preheated plates, sprinkling each portion with 2–3 pinches of dried bonito fish shavings (if using).

Spicy Thai chicken and rice vermicelli soup

Don't be daunted by the Thai spices and coconut milk. This is an incredibly simple and quick dish to prepare once you've acquired the ingredients – light and fresh and, of course, very tasty.

For 4–5 starter helpings, use:

> 1½ pints (850 ml) good chicken stock (see page 81)
> 4 fl oz (125 ml) tinned coconut milk
> 3 kaffir lime leaves, finely cut up with scissors
> 2 inches (5 cm) lemon grass, finely sliced
> 1 large spring onion, finely sliced
> 1 inch (½ cm) galangal (kha), finely chopped
> 1 tablespoon (1 × 15 ml spoon) light fish gravy
> 1 tablespoon (1 × 15 ml spoon) lemon juice
> 1 medium chicken breast (about 4 oz/100–125 g), boned and skinned
> ½ small dried red chilli (to taste), finely chopped
> 2 oz (50 g) cellophane noodles or rice vermicelli (dried)
> fresh coriander, chopped

Soak the rice vermicelli or cellophane noodles in cold water for half an hour. Drain.

Cut the chicken breast into half lengthways, then slice thinly. Heat the chicken stock, gently stir in the coconut milk, then add all the other ingredients except the chicken and the fresh coriander. Heat until it just begins to boil, then add the chicken. Simmer very gently until the chicken is cooked (2–3 minutes).

Meanwhile, put the vermicelli or noodles into a pan of boiling water for just 20–30 *seconds*, and drain. Vermicelli has a tendency to have a life of its own – one errant forkful can result in the whole lot following and landing on the floor, so I suggest putting the drained vermicelli on to a plate and cutting with a knife and fork into 3- to 4-inch (7–10-cm) segments.

Using delicate small bowls, put a ladleful of soup into each bowl, followed by some vermicelli and a sprinkling of chopped fresh coriander. Serve hot.

Thai spicy noodle soup with prawns and lettuce ○

An absolutely delicious, delicately flavoured clear soup. It is easy to make, attractive and very low in calories. Easily good enough to serve as a starter on a special occasion – if possible in white, or blue and white Oriental bowls. If you can't get hold of lemon grass or kaffir lime leaves, make the soup without. Use any kind of lettuce, or even thinly sliced Chinese or Savoy cabbage. If bean sprouts are unavailable, substitute extra lettuce.

Use Chinese egg noodles, which you can buy from any shop stocking Oriental ingredients and even some supermarkets, *or* use rice or cellophane noodles which you will find in the more specialized shops.

For 3–4 starter helpings, use:

> 1 tablespoon (1 × 15 ml spoon) nut or vegetable oil
> 2 cloves garlic, crushed
> ¼ small red chilli (to taste), broken into small pieces
> 2 teaspoons (2 × 5 ml spoons) grated fresh root ginger
> 1–2 spring onions, finely sliced
> a good pinch sea salt
> 4 oz (100–125 g) large prawns (about 10), cooked or raw
> 1½ pints (850 ml) good chicken stock
> 1 kaffir lime leaf, cut into slivers with kitchen scissors
> 2 inches (5 cm) lemon grass stalk, finely chopped
> 2 oz (50 g) lettuce, shredded
> 2 oz (50 g) bean sprouts
> 2 oz (50 g) button mushrooms (or 2–3 large shitake mushrooms), sliced
> 2–3 oz (50–100 g) Chinese egg noodles, *or* cellophane noodles

Like a good Oriental cook, first slice and chop your ingredients and have them ready on a large plate or board. If you wish, you can remove the shells of the prawns. Choose a saucepan big enough to hold the finished soup comfortably, or use a wok if you have one.

Stir fry the garlic, chilli, ginger and salt in the oil for just a few seconds. Add the prawns and continue to stir fry for under a minute. Pour over the chicken stock, add the lemon grass, lime leaf, lettuce and bean sprouts, and simmer for 10 minutes or so, adding the mushrooms just before the end.

Cook the noodles separately in plenty of boiling water for just a couple of minutes, watching carefully. Drain, and add to the soup just before serving. (If using rice/cellophane noodles, cook as directed on pages 9–11.)

Basmati rice with cardamom and fresh coriander

There is no point in pretending that these Oriental dishes can only be eaten with pasta. Most of them, of course, are equally good made with rice. The best type to use is undoubtedly Basmati rice, and this is my favourite way of cooking it. You can leave out the cardamom pods and coriander if you wish.

For 4–6 helpings, use:

> 12 oz (325 g) Basmati rice
> 2 tablespoons (2 × 15 ml spoons) nut or vegetable oil
> 1 oz (25 g) butter
> 8–10 cardamom pods (optional)
> 1¼ pints (⅔ litre) water
> sea salt
> 2–3 tablespoons (2–3 × 15 ml spoons) fresh coriander
>   (optional)

Put the rice into a sieve and rinse well with cold water, then put into a bowl, cover with water and soak for about 30 minutes. Drain well. Melt the butter with the oil over a low heat, then stir in the cardamom pods and cook for just a moment. Stir in the drained rice, then add the water with just a little salt.

Bring to the boil, then cover and allow to simmer on a *low* heat (as low as possible) for about 15 minutes, checking occasionally to make sure it hasn't boiled dry. When the rice is tender but not mushy, remove from the heat and drain off any excess water. Stir in the fresh chopped coriander (if using) and serve immediately.

Stir-fried chicken, peanuts and coriander with noodles

O

This dish was invented on the spur of the moment when my friend Nettie Mason appeared for a Thai dinner at my house, carrying her new-born baby in a basket. Although Nettie and her husband Nick adore hot, spicy food, it was felt that their baby might not appreciate an infusion of red and green chillies with kaffir lime leaves in his midnight feed.

Again, this is magically quick and easy.

For 2 modest main course helpings, use:

 1 tablespoon (1 × 15 ml spoon) nut or vegetable oil
 1 clove garlic, crushed
 1 chicken breast, boned and skinned (about 5 oz/150 g)
 ½ oz (15 g) roasted peanuts, crushed
 (O omit the peanuts)
 1 tablespoon (1 × 15 ml spoon) soy sauce
 1 tablespoon (1 × 15 ml spoon) chicken stock
 1 teaspoon (1 × 5 ml spoon) caster sugar
 1 teaspoon (1 × 5 ml spoon) fish sauce (optional)
 1 heaped tablespoon (1 × 15 ml spoon) fresh coriander, chopped
 4 oz (100–125 g) Chinese egg noodles

Cut the chicken breast into sections about 2 inches (5 cm) wide, then slice into thin strips.

Using a wok, if you have one, or else a medium-sized saucepan, stir fry the garlic in the oil in the bottom of the wok for just a few seconds. Throw in the chicken and stir fry, moving it almost continuously with a spatula, until the chicken is lightly browned/opaque on *all* surfaces. Add the soy sauce and sugar, then the chicken stock and the fish sauce (if using) and then the crushed peanuts, and continue to stir fry for a minute or so. (If you are cooking this dish in advance and reheating at the last moment, add a couple of extra spoons of chicken stock just before reheating.) Just before the noodles are ready, sprinkle over the fresh coriander.

Cook the Chinese noodles in plenty of salted boiling water for just a couple of minutes, taking great care not to overcook. Drain and then serve the noodles on a preheated plate, with the chicken and sauce on top; or serve separately, with the noodles (or rice) on the side.

Sweet and sour beef with black bean sauce, served with noodles

A very tasty but more conventional dish, for those who have not yet become addicted to the subtle flavours of Thai food. Extremely quick and easy to prepare.

For 2 modest main course helpings, use:

> 1 tablespoon (1 × 15 ml spoon) nut or vegetable oil
> 2 cloves garlic, crushed
> ¼–½ small dried red chilli (to taste), crumbled (optional)
> pinch sea salt
> 8 oz (225 g) sirloin or rump steak
> 1 tablespoon (1 × 15 ml spoon) soy sauce
> 1 dessertspoon (1 × 10 ml spoon) vinegar
> 1 heaped teaspoon (1 × 5 ml spoon) caster sugar
> 1½ tablespoons (1½ × 15 ml spoons) black bean sauce*
> 2 tablespoons (2 × 15 ml spoons) chicken stock
> 4 oz (100–125 g) Chinese noodles

Cut the steak lengthwise into two (leaving two pieces about 2 inches (5 cm) wide). Slice these pieces with the grain of the meat into slivers (about ¼ to ½ inch/½ to 1 cm thick).

Using a wok if you have one, or else a medium-sized saucepan, stir fry the garlic, chilli (if using) and salt in the oil in the bottom of the wok for just a few seconds. Throw in the beef and stir fry, moving the meat almost continuously with a spatula until it is lightly browned on *all* surfaces. Add the soy sauce, vinegar, chicken stock, black bean sauce and sugar, and continue to stir fry for half a minute. (If you are cooking this dish in advance and reheating at the last moment, add a couple of extra spoons of chicken stock just before reheating.)

---

* Easily found in any Oriental shop or even a large supermarket. Read the label carefully and try to avoid those with too many additives, in particular monosodium glutamate. I buy Sharwood's Stir Fry Black Bean Sauce from my local supermarket.

Cook the Chinese noodles in plenty of salted boiling water for just a couple of minutes, taking great care not to overcook. Serve the noodles on a preheated dish with the beef and sauce on top, or serve separately, with the noodles (or rice) on the side.

Thai egg noodles, stir fried with beef, soy sauce and kaffir lime leaves

The kaffir lime leaves (available only in Thai shops) add the most delicious and authentically Thai flavour to this dish. Remember, they can be stored frozen in a plastic bag in the deep freeze. A good way of turning a steak for one into a meal for two!

This recipe is equally tasty made with chicken breasts, and even with 2 oz (50 g) bean sprouts thrown in at the same time as the meat or chicken.

For 2 main course helpings, use:

1½ tablespoons (1½ × 15 ml spoons) nut or vegetable oil
1–2 cloves garlic, crushed
1 teaspoon (1 × 5 ml spoon) fresh root ginger, finely grated
2 kaffir lime leaves, finely cut up with scissors
4–6 oz (100–175 g) sirloin steak, thinly sliced
2 tablespoons (2 × 15 ml spoons) soy sauce
1 teaspoon (1 × 5 ml spoon) caster sugar
4 tablespoons (4 × 15 ml spoons) chicken stock
½–1 teaspoon (½–1 × 5 ml spoon) fish sauce (optional)
4 oz (100–125 g) Chinese egg noodles

Cut the steak lengthwise into two (leaving two pieces about 2 inches (5 cm) wide). Slice these pieces with the grain of the meat into slivers (about ¼ to ½ inch/½ to 1 cm thick).

In the bottom of a wok or a medium-sized pan, stir fry the garlic and the ginger in the oil for just a few seconds. Throw in the lime leaves and stir fry again for a few seconds. Add the sliced meat and stir fry, turning all the time, until the meat is lightly browned on all sides. Add the soy sauce, sugar, chicken stock and fish sauce (if using), and stir fry for another minute or so.

At the last moment, cook the Chinese noodles in plenty of salted boiling water for just a couple of minutes, taking great care not to overcook. Mix with the meat gently but thoroughly in the wok over a low heat. Serve immediately.

Stir-fried egg noodles with prawns, broccoli and coriander ○

A bright, fresh dish. Very good to eat and particularly healthy.

I use Chinese egg noodles, available in Oriental shops and in many good supermarkets, but this dish could also be made with cellophane noodles or rice sticks (see pages 9–11). The broccoli goes well with the prawns, but if it is not available you can substitute another vegetable. Go for something green and crisp – for example green beans, spinach, Chinese or Savoy cabbage, or even spring greens (finely sliced).

You could also add a beaten egg, tossing it together with the noodles and sauce over a low heat just before serving and before sprinkling over the coriander.

For 2 main course or 4 starter helpings, use:

> 1 tablespoon (1 × 15 ml spoon) vegetable or nut oil
> 1–2 cloves garlic, crushed
> ¼–½ dried red chilli, crumbled (to taste)
> 1 spring onion, finely chopped, *or* substitute 1 tablespoon
>   (1 × 15 ml spoon) finely chopped onion
> good pinch sea salt
> 1 tablespoon (1 × 15 ml spoon) soy sauce
> 2–3 tablespoons (2–3 × 15 ml spoons) chicken stock
> few drops fish sauce, to taste (optional)
> 4 oz (100–125 g) broccoli
> 4 oz (100–125 g) shelled cooked prawns
> 4 oz (100–125 g) Chinese egg noodles
> 2 tablespoons (2 × 15 ml spoons) fresh coriander, chopped

Put on your water for the pasta. While it is heating, prepare your other ingredients. As soon as the water boils, throw in the broccoli for just a couple of minutes. Remove with a slotted spoon, allow to cool a little, then slice lengthwise into bite-sized florets on little stalks. Cook the noodles until 'al dente' and transfer to a colander or sieve to drain while you stir fry the other ingredients.

Using a wok or a large frying pan, stir fry the garlic, chilli, spring onion or onion and salt in the oil for just a few seconds. Add the prawns and partially cooked broccoli and continue to stir fry for 20 seconds or so. Add the soy sauce, fish sauce and chicken stock, stir fry together, then mix in the drained noodles. Throw on the coriander, and toss together just once more. Serve immediately.

Oriental – fish, chicken and meat

Short macaroni with salmon and teriyaki sauce

A delicate, subtle dish with a slightly sweet yet also savoury taste which blends deliciously with the flavour of salmon. Some of the ingredients may sound a little exotic, but you will be pleased to hear that they are easily available in any shop stocking Japanese cooking ingredients. The Japanese do a particularly good soy sauce – light but flavoursome and naturally brewed – called Kikkoman Soy Sauce. If you do not have the time or energy to chase after these ingredients, I would recommend trying Bows with salmon or pink trout, soy sauce and sherry (page 137) – an anglicized version of this dish with slightly stronger flavour and colour.

Either of these dishes would go well with stir-fried Chinese cabbage but would also benefit from the strong colours and fresh taste of a large mixed salad or steamed green vegetables – for example broccoli and snow peas. Another idea would be to sprinkle some basil, chopped parsley or fresh coriander over the dish.

For 2 main course or 4 starter helpings, use:

3 tablespoons (3 × 15 ml spoons) soy sauce
3 tablespoons (3 × 15 ml spoons) sake
3 tablespoons (3 × 15 ml spoons) mirin
½ teaspoon (½ × 5 ml spoon) caster sugar
8 oz (225 g) salmon
6 oz (175 g) short macaroni or shells

Put the salmon in a small bowl, but one big enough for the salmon to lie flat. Mix together the soy sauce, sake, mirin and sugar and pour over the salmon. Leave to marinate for at least 5–10 minutes each side.

Poach the salmon very gently in its sauce for 3 minutes either side in a covered pan, so as to prevent the valuable juices from evaporating. Remove the fish with a fish slice, lay on a plate and flake coarsely, removing all skin and bones. (You will find that the fish will separate quite naturally into large flakes.) Do not be surprised if the fish seems translucent and still uncooked in the centre – this is intentional. The trick with salmon is not to overcook it, as it then loses its flavour. Allow the sauce to cool, then put the fish back in with the sauce while you prepare the pasta. At the last moment, gently reheat, adding a little water or white wine if necessary.

Cook the pasta in plenty of salted boiling water until 'al dente', drain, and put back into the pan. Pour over the fish and sauce, and mix together with the pasta over a low flame until heated through. Serve immediately on preheated plates, with definitely *no* cheese on the side!

Bows with salmon or pink trout, soy sauce and sherry

An anglicized version of the previous recipe, using more easily obtainable ingredients. The result is delicious, a little stronger in colour and flavour, with the taste of the soy sauce more obvious. With both these recipes you can take advantage of the cheaper 'farmed' salmon and pink trout, or even use a salmon tail, but do remember to buy enough to take into account the wastage in the form of skin and bones.

For 2 main course or 4 starter helpings, use:

> 3 tablespoons (3 × 15 ml spoons) soy sauce
> 3 tablespoons (3 × 15 ml spoons) light dry sherry or dry vermouth
> 3 tablespoons (3 × 15 ml spoons) water
> 1 teaspoon (1 × 5 ml spoon) caster sugar
> 8 oz (225 g) salmon
> 6 oz (175 g) bows

Put the salmon in a small bowl, but one big enough for the salmon to lie flat. Mix together the soy sauce, sherry or vermouth, water and sugar and pour over the salmon. Leave to marinate for at least 5–10 minutes each side.

Poach the salmon very gently in its sauce for 3 minutes either side in a covered pan, so as to prevent the valuable juices from evaporating. Remove the fish with a fish slice, lay on a plate and flake coarsely, removing all skin and bones. (You will find that the fish will separate quite naturally into large flakes.) The fish should be slightly undercooked in the centre as overcooking salmon will cause it to lose its flavour. Allow the sauce to cool, then put the fish back in with the sauce while you prepare the pasta. At the last moment, gently reheat, adding a little water or white wine if necessary.

Cook the pasta in plenty of salted boiling water until 'al dente', drain, and put back into the pan. Pour over the fish and sauce, and mix together with the pasta over a low flame until heated through. Serve immediately on preheated plates, with definitely *no* cheese on the side!

Wholewheat shells with stir-fried crab, ginger, fennel, coriander and optional garlic croûtons

You can use wholewheat or plain pasta for this dish. The croûtons and the coriander give the dish its colour as well as extra flavour, but you could leave them out, especially if you elect to use a coloured pasta – either wholewheat or one of the orange-red or green pastas now available.

For 3–4 main course helpings, use:

> 2 tablespoons (2 × 15 ml spoons) sesame, vegetable or nut oil
> 2 teaspoons (2 × 5 ml spoons) fresh root ginger, finely grated
> ¾ inch (1 cm) dried chilli, finely chopped
> 3 cloves garlic, crushed
> sea salt
> 1 tablespoon (1 × 15 ml spoons) shallots or spring onions, finely chopped
> 1 head fennel (about 6–8 oz/175–225 g), very finely sliced
> 1 tin (6 oz/170 g) crab in brine, drained
> 2 tablespoons (2 × 15 ml spoons) fresh coriander, finely chopped
> 2 tablespoons (2 × 15 ml spoons) white wine
> 2 tablespoons (2 × 15 ml spoons) chicken stock, fresh or made with a pinch of chicken stock cube and water
> 9–12 oz (250–350 g) wholewheat, plain or coloured pasta shells or shapes
> extra 2 tablespoons (2 × 15 ml spoons) sesame or other oil

For the croûtons

> 2 oz (50 g) bread, cut into small cubes
> 2 cloves garlic, crushed
> 1½ tablespoons (1½ × 15 ml spoons) nut or vegetable oil

Use a wok if you have one, or else a frying pan large enough to take the pasta and sauce. If you have a food processor with a very fine slicing blade (for stir-fried vegetables), use that for slicing the fennel, or else slice it by hand with a sharp knife.

Sauté the chilli, shallots or spring onions, half the ginger and two cloves of crushed garlic with a good pinch of sea salt in the sesame or other oil. Throw in the sliced fennel and stir fry for several minutes. (That is, fry on a fairly high heat, keeping the contents of the wok or pan constantly moving with a wooden spatula or spoon.) Add the wine and allow to bubble for half a minute, then add the chicken stock. Set aside until the pasta and croûtons are ready.

To make the croûtons, fry the bread cubes in the oil and crushed garlic. (The bread will absorb the oil very quickly.) Keep on frying until the croûtons are golden, or browned.

Meanwhile, cook the pasta in plenty of salted boiling water until 'al dente'. Drain, put back into the pan and toss with the extra oil and the remaining ginger and clove of crushed garlic. Add the pasta to the wok or frying pan with the sauce, add the drained tinned crab, and heat together over a low flame until heated through. Transfer to a preheated serving dish (or serve directly from the wok), sprinkle over the coriander and croûtons, and serve immediately.

Chinese good fortune New Year noodles with cabbage and prawns or crab meat

Last year I spent the Chinese New Year in Hong Kong with my husband and his children. The Regent Hotel, where we were staying, gave a New Year Banquet in our honour, and as their Chinese restaurant is undoubtedly one of the best in the world, this feast was indeed an occasion to remember.

There was another event which caused the evening to be particularly memorable. Before the dinner began, two men came into the room carrying a wicker basket. The guests crowded round as they opened the basket and revealed the contents: three deadly poisonous snakes. Coward that I am, I beat a hasty retreat to the furthest corner of the room. One of the men picked up a snake and ran it through his hands. Eventually he found what he was looking for. He reached for a razor and made a small slit in the snake's stomach, about two-thirds of the way along its body. From this hole he drew a small brown ball on a string – the snake's gall bladder – and placed this strange object on the side of a plate. This macabre exercise was repeated until there were three miniature balloons across the side of the plate. The unhappy snakes were then returned to the basket, and the gall bladders were taken to be mashed up with some rice wine. We, as honoured guests of this evening, were then presented with glasses of this liquid. It would keep us in good health for years, we were told. Etiquette prevailing, we drained the cups with hardly a grimace.

For 3–4 light main course helpings, use:

> 2 tablespoons (2 × 15 ml spoons) vegetable or nut oil
> pinch sea salt
> 8 oz (225 g) Chinese, green or Savoy cabbage, very finely
>   sliced
> 1 clove garlic, crushed (optional)
> 8 oz (225 g) cooked shelled shrimps or prawns,
>   *or* 7 oz (200 g) tin crab meat
> 2 tablespoons (2 × 15 ml spoons) sake (rice wine) or pale

dry sherry
2 tablespoons (2 × 15 ml spoons) soy sauce
1 scant teaspoon (1 × 5 ml spoon) caster sugar
6 tablespoons (6 × 15 ml spoons) strong fresh chicken
    stock
6 oz (175 g) Chinese noodles

Put on the water for the noodles. While it is heating, prepare the other ingredients.

Put the oil into a hot wok or large frying pan, then throw in the finely sliced cabbage, salt and garlic (if using). Stir fry the cabbage and garlic in the oil for a minute or so, then add the prawns (if you are using prawns) and continue to stir fry for half a minute. Add the sake, soy sauce and sugar, stir fry for a few seconds, then add the chicken stock and continue to toss the contents of the pan until well mixed. Turn off the heat and quickly cook the noodles in plenty of salted boiling water for just a couple of minutes until *almost* ready. Drain, then add them to the contents of the wok. Mix together gently, allowing the underdone noodles to absorb the juices and adding a little more chicken stock if necessary. At the last moment, add the tinned crab meat (if using) and stir together gently until well heated through. Serve immediately.

Thai white fish with courgettes, noodles and spicy green sauce

This pale green Thai 'curry' sauce is, in my experience, the most exquisite and universally popular of all Thai tastes. It *is* possible to make these curry pastes yourself, but as you will have to buy a few essential items of Thai ingredients before venturing on any Thai dish, it makes sense to stock up on a few packets of the red and green curry pastes (see page 15) and store them in your fridge. For a simpler version of the sauce, all that is really required is a spoonful of paste and a little tinned coconut milk – although as you can see, in these recipes I have gone the whole hog and added a few more irresistibly delicious ingredients.

In this recipe the fish is cooked carefully in the oven in order to retain clearly discernible pieces of fish *with* sauce, rather than allowing it to deteriorate into a mush! When I cooked this dish for some friends, one of them actually mistook the succulent chunks of this comparatively inexpensive cut of haddock for scallops.

I would serve this with some strongly coloured stir-fried or steamed vegetables – for example broccoli, spinach, courgettes – and, if possible, some miniature corn on the cobs. It would also go equally well with a plate of Basmati rice (see page 124) as with pasta.

For 3–4 main course helpings, use:

> 1 tablespoon (1 × 15 ml spoons) nut or vegetable oil
> 1 clove garlic, crushed
> 1 tablespoon (1 × 15 ml spoon) green curry paste
> 6 fl oz (175 ml) tinned coconut milk
> 3 fl oz (90 ml) water
> 1 tablespoon (1 × 15 ml spoon) fresh root ginger, grated
> 1 tablespoon (1 × 15 ml spoon) galangal, finely chopped
> 1 tablespoon (1 × 15 ml spoon) fish sauce (optional)
> 2 kaffir lime leaves, finely chopped with scissors
> 1 teaspoon (1 × 5 ml spoon) palm sugar (or substitute one
>   generous teaspoon thick honey or sugar)

6 oz (175 g) courgettes, sliced
12 oz (325–350 g) firm white fish, e.g. haddock or cod
  (weighed without skin)
8 oz (225 g) Chinese egg noodles
2–4 tablespoons (2–4 × 15 ml spoons) fresh coriander,
  chopped

Pour the coconut milk into a bowl and beat with a fork or
spoon until the creamy part is well integrated with the thinner
liquid. Measure out the 6 fl oz (175 ml) into another small
bowl, and beat together with the water. Put aside.

Put the curry paste with the garlic and oil in the bottom of a
pan and stir over a low heat until the paste is well mixed with
the oil. Stir in the coconut milk and water. Add the ginger,
fish sauce (if using), galangal, lime leaves and palm sugar, and
stir together. Simmer over a low heat for a few minutes to let
the ingredients infuse, then add the courgettes. Cook for
another 5 minutes.

If the fish has not already been skinned by the fishmonger,
skin it yourself. Lay it on a chopping board skin side down.
Hold the thin/tail end in your left hand and slice away from
yourself, using the leverage against the board to remove the
fish from the skin as cleanly as possible.

Put the fish in a shallow ovenproof dish just large enough to
hold it and the sauce. Pour the sauce over, and cook in a
preheated oven (375°F/190°C/gas mark 5) for about 15 minutes,
until the fish is cooked but still firm.

Meanwhile, cook the Chinese noodles in plenty of salted
boiling water for just a few minutes, watching them carefully,
until cooked (but not too soft), remembering to stir well at the
onset to separate the noodles. Drain.

Put the noodles on a flat, preheated serving dish, and slide
the fish and sauce over the top. Break up the fish gently with a
wooden spoon so as to distribute it evenly but not to destroy
the texture. Sprinkle with the chopped coriander and serve
immediately, or serve separately, with the noodles (or rice) on
the side.

Thai white fish with prawns, crushed peanuts, noodles and spicy red sauce

Cook as for Thai white fish with courgettes, noodles and spicy green sauce (see previous recipe), substituting 1 tablespoon (1 × 15 ml spoon) red curry paste for the green curry paste, and 4 oz (100–125 g) cooked and shelled prawns or shrimps for the courgettes, and replacing the chopped coriander with 2 oz (50 g) crushed roasted peanuts, sprinkled over the dish just before serving.

Serve as above, with noodles, or serve separately, with noodles (or rice) on the side.

Stir-fried noodles with crab meat, asparagus and optional crispy bacon

Another Oriental 'staple'. Be adventurous and experiment, using this recipe as a basic standard. You could use smoked chicken or avocado instead of the bacon, and prawns or leftover cold salmon instead of crab meat. If you have grown to appreciate the surprisingly subtle qualities of fish gravy, you may want to use a spoonful in this dish. Or you could beat up a raw egg and throw it on at the last moment, just before the crab, allowing it to 'scramble' in the wok along with the other ingredients. Another variation would be to use rice or cellophane noodles instead of Chinese egg noodles.

For 2 main course helpings, use:

>   2–4 slices (2 oz/50 g) smoked bacon, finely cut if possible
>   1½ tablespoons (1½ × 15 ml spoons) nut or vegetable oil
>   pinch sea salt
>   1–2 cloves garlic, crushed
>   1 large or 2 small spring onions, finely sliced
>   1 teaspoon (1 × 5 ml spoon) fresh root ginger, finely grated
>   ¼ dried red chilli, finely crumbled (optional)
>   8 oz (225 g) fresh asparagus, *or* substitute broccoli or 4 oz (100–125 g) mange-tout (snow peas)
>   3 tablespoons (3 × 15 ml spoons) fresh strong chicken stock
>   5 oz (150 g) Chinese egg noodles
>   1 tin (7 oz/200 g) crab in brine, drained

Grill the bacon until crispy and leave in a low oven on a piece of kitchen roll to keep warm. At the last moment, cut into little pieces using kitchen scissors.

Put on your water for the pasta. While it is heating, prepare your vegetables. Cut off the coarse part of the spears from the asparagus or the stalks from the broccoli, or the ends from the mange-tout (pulling off the 'string' down the side at the same time). As soon as the water boils, throw in the asparagus or broccoli for just a couple of minutes, or the mange-tout for less than a minute. Remove the vegetable with a slotted spoon, allow to cool a little, then cut asparagus into 1-inch ($\frac{1}{2}$-cm) sections, slice broccoli lengthwise into bite-sized florets on little stalks, or slice mange-tout diagonally, each one into three. Prepare all the other ingredients as directed and leave out ready near the stove, cooking the noodles quickly – for just a couple of minutes – as you stir fry the other ingredients.

Using a wok or large frying pan, stir fry the garlic, chilli, spring onion, ginger and salt in the oil for just a few seconds. Add the parboiled green vegetable and continue to stir fry for a minute or so. Pour on the chicken stock, stir fry together, then mix in the drained noodles. At the last moment, add the crab meat and stir together gently until heated through. Sprinkle on the bacon pieces (if using) and then serve immediately.

Chinese noodles with rich and spicy chicken and red pepper sauce ○

This recipe started out as a Korean chicken stew, but with the addition of a few extras grew into something quite different. The marinating of the chicken in the rich soy sauce gives it a gamey flavour. One of the lunch guests sampling this dish actually thought it might have been a very tender piece of venison!

For 2–3 main course helpings, use:

$\frac{1}{2}$ tablespoon ($\frac{1}{2}$ × 15 ml spoon) sesame seed oil
2 tablespoons (2 × 15 ml spoons) soy sauce
2 tablespoons (2 × 15 ml spoons) sake (rice wine) or pale dry sherry
2 tablespoons (2 × 15 ml spoons) chicken stock
1 teaspoon (1 × 5 ml spoon) sugar
$\frac{1}{4}$ dried red chilli, to taste
2 cloves garlic, crushed
2 spring onions, finely sliced
1 teaspoon (1 × 5 ml spoon) fresh root ginger, grated
1 teaspoon (1 × 5 ml spoon) damson preserve or redcurrant jelly
$\frac{1}{4}$ sweet red pepper (2 oz/50 g), finely sliced
6–8 oz (175–225 g) chicken (weighed without skin or bone), breast or leg, or a piece of each
6 oz (175 g) Chinese egg noodles

Mix all the ingredients except the chicken and noodles in a small bowl. Cut the chicken into small bite-sized pieces and put into the bowl with the sauce. Marinate for a couple of hours at room temperature (or 8 hours/overnight in the fridge).

Put the chicken and marinade into a small pan and stew gently for about 20 minutes, or until the chicken is tender.

Meanwhile, cook the noodles in plenty of salted boiling water until softened. Drain, and return to the pan with the cooked chicken sauce. Serve immediately.

Green Thai spicy chicken with coconut milk, served with noodles

This is really my all-time favourite Thai dish. Although very spicy, it is delicate in colour and flavour. Don't be put off by the length of the list of ingredients, or their unfamiliarity. This dish is really extremely simple and surprisingly quick to prepare, once you have made the initial trip to the Thai shop.

The recipe was first given to me by a friend, Katie Page. She and her husband Nat lived in Bangkok for three years. Katie is one of those wonderful cooks who creates feasts for twelve at a day's notice, and when you arrive at her house the kitchen is *so* tidy that you find yourself rather nervously enquiring if you have come on the right night!

An excellent dish to serve at a dinner party – although only to friends who enjoy spicy food! For six to eight people, use six chicken breasts and simply treble the other ingredients. Or, even better, make enough for four (double quantities) and serve with another Thai dish (for example 'Thai Muslim' beef coconut curry, page 160). Serve with a big plate of steamed broccoli, mange-tout, courgettes, and any other vegetables which look good in the shop, and with noodles or Basmati rice.

For 2–3 main course helpings, use:

> 1 tablespoon (1 × 15 ml spoon) nut or vegetable oil
> 1 clove garlic, crushed
> ½ small dried red chilli (to taste), crumbled (optional)
> 1 tablespoon (1 × 15 ml spoon) green curry paste
> 2 chicken breasts (about 10 oz/275 g), skinned and boned, chopped into chunks the size of a double sugar lump
> 7 fl oz (200 ml) tinned coconut milk
> 2 fl oz (50 ml) chicken stock or water
> 2 spring onions, finely sliced
> 1 tablespoon (1 × 15 ml spoon) fresh root ginger, grated or finely chopped
> 1 inch (2½ cm) galangal, peeled and sliced into thin rounds
> ½ tablespoon (½ × 15 ml spoon) fish sauce (optional)

3 kaffir lime leaves, finely chopped with scissors
2 inches (5 cm) lemon grass, finely sliced
1 teaspoon (1 × 5 ml spoon) palm sugar (or substitute one
   generous teaspoon thick honey or sugar)
about 20 pea aubergines* (scant 1 oz/25 g) (optional)
4 oz (100–125 g) small round green aubergines*, halved, or
   4 oz (100–125 g) Mediterranean aubergine, thickly sliced,
   drained (see page 57) and cut into quarters
4 oz (100–125 g) Chinese egg noodles
2–4 tablespoons (2–4 × 15 ml spoons) coriander, chopped

Pour the coconut milk into a bowl and beat with a fork or
spoon until the creamy part is well integrated with the thinner
liquid. Measure out the 7 fl oz (200 ml) into another small bowl
or measuring jug, and beat together with the stock or water.
Put aside.

Sauté the garlic and chilli (if using) in the oil in the bottom of
a medium-sized saucepan over a low flame for just a few
seconds. Add the curry paste and continue to stir until mixed
together with the oil. Add the chicken pieces and sauté in the
mixture for a couple of minutes. Add the coconut milk and
water and stir together well, still over a low flame. Add the
spring onion, ginger, galangal, fish sauce (if using), lime
leaves, lemon grass, pea aubergines (if available) and palm
sugar, and stir together. Simmer for 5 minutes, then add the
larger aubergine. Simmer for another 20 minutes, or until the
chicken is well softened.

At the last moment, cook the Chinese noodles in plenty of
salted boiling water for just a couple of minutes, taking great
care not to overcook. Mix chicken, sauce and noodles together
gently on a preheated dish, sprinkle over the chopped
coriander, and serve immediately, or serve chicken separately,
with the noodles (or rice) on the side.

* Little green aubergines, almost as small as peas, with a slightly peppery taste.
Not one of the essentials of Thai cuisine but very nice in this dish, if you can get
hold of some. Both these and the round green aubergines are usually available at
Thai provision stores.

Stir-fried chicken and pork with bean sprouts, Chinese cabbage and noodles

A very tasty noodle dish which will not shock the palates of those with more conventional tastes! You could, of course, use all chicken or all pork instead of mixing the two – and, by the same token, all bean sprouts or Chinese cabbage. If you cannot find either, use any type of cabbage or even lettuce, sliced very finely.

For 2–3 main course helpings, use:

> 2 tablespoons (2 × 15 ml spoons) vegetable or nut oil
> 1 clove garlic, crushed
> ¼ dried red chilli (to taste), crumbled or finely chopped
> 1 teaspoon (1 × 5 ml spoon) fresh root ginger, grated
> 1 small (3 oz/75–100 g meat only) chicken breast
> 1 small pork escalope or chop (3 oz/75–100 g meat only),
>   very finely sliced, *or* 3 oz (75–100 g) minced pork
> 4 oz (100–125 g) firm bean curd, cut into small squares
> 4 oz (100–125 g) bean sprouts
> 4 oz (100–125 g) Chinese cabbage, very finely sliced
> 1 tablespoon (1 × 15 ml spoon) soy sauce
> ½ tablespoon (½ × 15 ml spoon) vinegar
> 1 teaspoon (1 × 5 ml spoon) fish sauce (optional)
> 2 tablespoons (2 × 15 ml spoons) chicken stock
> 1 teaspoon (1 × 5 ml spoon) caster sugar
> 4 oz (100–125 g) Chinese noodles
> 1 oz (25 g) roasted peanuts, crushed (see page 16)
> 2 tablespoons (2 × 15 ml spoons) coriander, chopped
>   (optional)

Stir fry the ginger, garlic and chilli in half the oil. Add the chicken and pork and stir fry until all the surfaces are opaque/ lightly browned. Add the bean curd, bean sprouts and cabbage and the remaining spoon of oil, and continue to stir fry for a minute or so or until the vegetables soften a little. Add the soy sauce, fish sauce (if using), vinegar, sugar and chicken stock, one at a time, and continue to stir fry for a minute or so.

At the last moment, cook the Chinese noodles in plenty of salted boiling water for just a couple of minutes, taking great care not to overcook. Mix together with the chicken gently but thoroughly in the wok over a low heat. Sprinkle the crushed peanuts and coriander (if using) over the dish on the serving plate just before putting on the table.

Sanuk's stir-fried rice vermicelli with pork, coriander, bean curd, bean sprouts, red pepper and peanuts

I think the best Thai food I have ever eaten has been in the house of some friends of mine, Benny and Axel Alewyn. (Axel is the author of the blockbuster *The Falcon of Siam*, a novel set in seventeenth-century Thailand.) They now live in a romantic castle in Scotland, and Thai food is served at every meal except breakfast. Not surprisingly, people travel hundreds of miles just to dine with them! They have the good fortune not only to have lived for many years in Thailand, but to have as their cook a very talented Thai lady called Sanuk. The following is one of her many 'specials'.

Do not be deterred by the long list of ingredients. The idea is to make a tasty meal and have fun doing it. (*Sanuk* means 'fun' in Thai.) Most of the ingredients in this recipe are optional, or at least interchangeable with whatever else you can find of a similar nature. Sanuk makes a variation of this dish using fresh crab meat instead of pork. You could also substitute chicken.

For 3–4 main course helpings, use:

> 2 tablespoons (2 × 15 ml spoons) nut or vegetable oil
> 2 cloves garlic, crushed
> 1 dried red chilli (to taste), crumbled into tiny pieces
> 4 tablespoons (4 × 15 ml spoons) fresh coriander, finely chopped
> 6 oz (175 g) pork, minced *or* pork steak, finely sliced
> ½ sweet red pepper, finely sliced
> ½ oz (15 g) dried shrimps, lightly crushed (optional)
> 2 oz (50 g) bean sprouts
> 4 spring onions (green part only), sliced
> 4 oz (100–125 g) firm bean curd, cut into small squares
> ½ tablespoon (½ × 15 ml spoon) fish sauce
> ½ tablespoon (½ × 15 ml spoon) vinegar
> 1 tablespoon (1 × 15 ml spoon) soy sauce

1½ teaspoons (1½ × 5 ml spoons) caster sugar
4 tablespoons (4 × 15 ml spoons) chicken stock or water
1½ oz (40 g) roasted peanuts, crushed
3½ oz (100 g) dried rice vermicelli
1 egg, beaten (optional)

Soak the rice vermicelli in cold water for half an hour, then drain. Put into a pan of boiling water for just 20–30 *seconds*, and drain again. (Vermicelli can be awkward to handle – I would suggest putting the drained vermicelli on to a plate and cutting with a knife and fork into 3- to 4-inch/7–10-cm segments.) Put to one side.

As stir frying is such a fast-moving, labour-intensive process, it is essential to prepare all the ingredients in advance and lay them out on a large chopping board or plate, and to place containers of liquids and measuring spoons within easy reach. Prepare all ingredients as directed. Make sure the peanuts are well roasted and crunchy. If not, then put on a baking tray in a hot oven until lightly browned (probably about 10–15 minutes). To crush them, place them in a plastic bag and beat them on a chopping board with a rolling pin. Lightly crush the dried shrimps in the same way.

Stir fry the garlic, chilli and half the chopped coriander in half the oil for just a few seconds. Throw in the pork and continue to stir fry until the meat is browned all over. Add the red pepper, bean sprouts, spring onions and the rest of the oil and continue to stir fry for a couple of minutes, or until the vegetables being to soften. Add the soy sauce, fish sauce and vinegar, and sprinkle on the sugar. Stir fry for a few seconds, then add the chicken stock or water and stir fry for a further 10 seconds or so. Stir in the beaten egg (if using), then add the bean curd and stir fry, turning more gently now. Add the noodles, mix together over the heat, and serve immediately, sprinkling over the peanuts and remaining coriander just before serving.

If there is any left over, don't throw it away. This dish is just as good eaten cold.

Linguini with lamb kidneys and teriyaki sauce

I adore lamb kidneys; they are not only very tasty but especially nutritious, and very good value for money. I find that the teriyaki sauce goes particularly well with them. Serve with a green vegetable or salad, and you'll have a very nourishing and delectable meal.

For 2 main course helpings, use:

> 2 tablespoons (2 × 15 ml spoons) nut or vegetable oil
> 1 tablespoon (1 × 15 ml spoon) olive oil
> 2 cloves garlic, crushed
> 1 tablespoon (1 × 15 ml spoon) onion or spring onion, very finely chopped
> 2 teaspoons (2 × 5 ml spoons) fresh root ginger, finely chopped or grated
> $\frac{1}{4}$ inch ($\frac{3}{4}$ cm) dried red chilli, finely chopped
> sea salt
> 6 oz (175 g) lamb kidneys (about 3)
> freshly ground black pepper
> 6 oz (175 g) linguini or spaghetti

For the sauce

> $1\frac{1}{2}$ tablespoons ($1\frac{1}{2}$ × 15 ml spoons) soy sauce
> 2 tablespoons (2 × 15 ml spoons) sake, white wine, dry sherry or vermouth
> 1 teaspoon (1 × 5 ml spoon) caster sugar
> 4 tablespoons (4 × 15 ml spoons) chicken stock

Prepare the kidneys by removing the membrane surrounding the meat and slicing into thin slices, cutting out and discarding the tough central sinew with kitchen scissors. Mix the sauce ingredients together in a cup and put aside.

Sauté the onion, ginger, chilli, a pinch of sea salt and one of the cloves of garlic in the nut or vegetable oil over a fairly high heat for just 1 minute. Throw in the prepared kidneys and stir fry with a wooden spoon or spatula for barely a minute until the kidneys are *just* cooked but still tender. (Do bear in mind that kidneys go a little chewy and hard if overcooked, and that you will be cooking them a little more in the later stages.) Pour on the sauce, and cook for a further half a minute, stirring the kidneys with a wooden spoon and allowing the sauce just to bubble (no longer than half a minute or the sauce will reduce too much). Turn off the heat, remove the kidneys with a slotted spoon and put aside.

Meanwhile, cook the pasta in plenty of salted boiling water until 'al dente'. Drain, and put back into the wok or saucepan with the sauce. At the last moment, while the pasta is cooking, toss the kidneys quickly in a small pan in the olive oil with the remaining clove of garlic. Season. Heat the pasta and sauce together in the wok, stirring continuously. Add the kidneys, toss together, and serve immediately, piping hot.

Salopian spicy fried beef with rice noodles

I found this exquisite dish in the countryside outside Adelaide in Australia. On a very stormy night our intrepid hosts took us out for a bite to the local 'pub'. It turned out to be the most charming country restaurant called The Salopian Inn. We found ourselves in a simple whitewashed room with a glorious blazing log fire, and at one end a virtually open-plan kitchen in which the young chef, Russell Jeavons, was creating his masterpieces of invention combining Oriental with European cuisine.

For 4 main course helpings, use:

1 tablespoon (1 × 15 ml spoon) butter or ghee
2 tablespoons (2 × 15 ml spoons) nut or vegetable oil
pinch sea salt
6 oz (175 g) onion, finely chopped
2 cloves garlic, crushed
1 tablespoon (1 × 15 ml spoon) fresh root ginger, grated
1 tablespoon (1 × 15 ml spoon) strong tamarind juice* (or
    substitute 2 tablespoons/2 × 15 ml spoons lemon juice)
1 tablespoon (1 × 15 ml spoon) tomato sauce (ketchup, or
    a scant tablespoon/15 ml spoon tomato concentrate)
1 tablespoon (1 × 15 ml spoon) soy sauce
1 lb (450 g) beef sirloin or filet, sliced into flat thin pieces,
    about 1 inch (2½ cm) square *or* use leftover cold beef
1 very small dried red chilli, crumbled (optional),
    or ¼ teaspoon (¼ × 5 ml spoon) chilli powder
12 oz (325–350 g) combination of 3 different sorts of stir-fry
    vegetables, very finely sliced, e.g. Chinese cabbage,
    Savoy cabbage, spinach, bean sprouts, blanched
    broccoli, mange-tout (snow peas), mushrooms, red
    pepper, etc.

---

* Buy a block of tamarind from an Oriental or Indian grocer. (It looks very much like a packet of dried dates.) Break off a piece about the size of a large prune. Put in a very small saucepan, pour boiling water over it (just enough to cover) and simmer on a low heat for a few minutes, breaking it up and mashing it with a wooden spoon as it begins to soften. Strain, and use.

4 oz (100–125 g) rice noodles (rice sticks – dried flat ribbon noodles), or substitute Chinese noodles

2 tablespoons (2 × 15 ml spoons) fresh coriander, chopped

Sauté the onion in the butter with the salt until softened and turning golden. Add the garlic and ginger and continue to cook, stirring frequently, until the ingredients are well softened. Add the tamarind juice, tomato sauce and soy sauce, and cook for a couple of minutes more. Put aside.

Soak the rice noodles briefly in near-boiling water until they are not quite tender. The final cooking with the other ingredients will finish them off.

If using uncooked beef, using a wok or heavy-based pan, sauté the meat in a tablespoon (15 ml spoon) of the oil (and the chilli, if using) over a high heat until lightly browned all over, and set aside on a plate before the juices start to run. Put the remaining spoon of oil in the wok. Stir fry the vegetables for a minute or so, then add the onion mixture and continue to stir fry for a couple of minutes. Add the noodles and cook for about 2 minutes, moving the whole lot vigorously round the pan. Add the beef (if using leftovers, add them now) and heat through thoroughly. Serve with freshly chopped coriander sprinkled on top.

Red Thai spicy beef with coconut milk and red pepper, served with noodles

Although this dish is based on the idea of a classical Thai curry, I hesitate to use the word 'curry' because of its associations with Indian restaurants. The Thai curry, although spicy, is exquisitely delicate in flavour, texture and appearance in comparison with its Indian counterpart (although some Indians might disagree).

This is an absolute favourite with everybody, especially when you are in the mood for something spicy. Again, don't be put off by the exotic-sounding ingredients. A visit to a Thai shop will provide you with everything except the beef.

You don't have to serve this dish with noodles; it goes equally well with Basmati rice (see page 124).

For 2 main course helpings, use:

> 1 tablespoon (1 × 15 ml spoon) nut or vegetable oil
> 1 clove garlic, crushed
> 1 tablespoon (1 × 15 ml spoon) red curry paste
> 4 fl oz (125 ml) tinned coconut milk
> 4 fl oz (125 ml) water
> 2 kaffir lime leaves, cut into slivers with kitchen scissors
> ¼ large red pepper, thinly sliced
> 4 oz (100–125 g) sirloin steak
> 1 teaspoon (1 × 5 ml spoon) galangal (kha), finely chopped
> ½ tablespoon (½ × 15 ml spoon) light fish gravy
> 1 teaspoon (1 × 5 ml spoon) palm sugar, or substitute thick honey or sugar
> 4 small round aubergines, cut into quarters,* or 3 oz (75–100 g) Mediterranean aubergine, thickly sliced, drained (page 57) and slices cut into quarters, or 3 oz (75–100 g) courgettes, thickly sliced, slices cut into quarters
> 6 oz (175 g) Chinese egg noodles

* These green aubergines should be available in Thai shops.

Pour the coconut milk into a bowl and beat the contents with a fork or spoon until the creamy part is well integrated with the thinner liquid. Measure out the 4 fl oz (125 ml) into another small bowl, and beat together with the water. Put aside.

Sauté the garlic in the oil in the bottom of a medium-sized saucepan over a low flame for just a few seconds. Add the curry paste and continue to stir until mixed together with the oil. Add the coconut milk and water and stir together well, still over a low heat. Add the red pepper slices and simmer gently for about 10 minutes to soften them.

Cut the steak lengthwise into two (leaving two pieces about 2 inches/5 cm wide). Slice these pieces with the grain of the meat into slivers (about $\frac{1}{4}$ to $\frac{1}{2}$ inch/$\frac{1}{2}$ to 1 cm thick). Add the sliced meat, chopped galangal, fish gravy, sugar and aubergines or courgettes to the contents of the saucepan and simmer for another 20 minutes. (This sauce with meat can be made in advance and reheated just before adding to the pasta and serving.)

At the last moment, cook the Chinese noodles in plenty of salted boiling water for just a couple of minutes, taking great care not to overcook. Mix gently with the sauce on a preheated dish, and serve immediately, or serve separately, with the noodles (or rice) on the side.

'Thai Muslim' beef coconut curry with noodles

A very easy, very tasty curry which I first sampled at one of my favourite Thai restaurants, the Blue Elephant in Fulham Road in London. Only in three other restaurants have I eaten such delicious food: the Asian Gateway in Darwin, Northern Australia, the Bangkok in Sydney, and the Lemon Grass in Bangkok.

For 2 main course helpings, use:

> 1 tablespoon (1 × 15 ml spoon) nut or vegetable oil
> 2 cloves garlic, crushed
> 1 tablespoon (1 × 15 ml spoon) Thai Matsaman curry paste*
> 7 fl oz (200 ml) tinned coconut milk
> 8–10 oz (225–275 g) rump steak, cut into chunks the size of a double sugar lump
> 6 cardamom pods, crushed with the handle of a knife
> 1 teaspoon (1 × 5 ml spoon) ground cinnamon
> 1 teaspoon (1 × 5 ml spoon) palm sugar, *or* substitute honey
> 2 tablespoons (2 × 15 ml spoons) tamarind juice (see page 156), *or* substitute lime or lemon juice
> 4 oz (100–125 g) Chinese noodles
> 1 oz (25 g) roasted peanuts, crushed

In a medium-sized saucepan, sauté the garlic gently in the oil for a few seconds. Add the curry paste and mix together well, then stir in the coconut milk. Add the cardamom pods, cinnamon, palm sugar, tamarind juice and meat, stir well, then simmer on a very low heat for about 40 minutes, adding the peanuts towards the end.

Just before the sauce is ready, cook the Chinese noodles in plenty of salted boiling water for only a couple of minutes, taking care not to overcook. Serve the meat and sauce on a bed of noodles (or alternatively serve with rice).

* Again, available at Thai provision stores. It looks like the red curry paste, so be sure to read the label carefully.

Oriental – vegetarian

Green Thai aubergine coconut curry

I'm usually put off using aubergines because they seem to drink up so much oil in the cooking, which boosts the calories in the dish! In this dish, however, we steam them first, which softens them beautifully without adding a single calorie.

This is a vegetarian version of the famous Thai green coconut curry. It is a very subtle dish – a delicate grey, with the seeds and the black slices of aubergine skin producing a decorative and pleasing effect. As with all coconut curries it is quite rich, and people who have never eaten Thai food might find the taste a little unusual; so if you are making a vegetarian meal for friends, I would suggest serving it with something more straightforward, such as Lentil lasagne (page 54), and lots of steamed vegetables for colour.

Use either Chinese egg noodles or noodles made from rice (see page 11).

For 2 main course or 4 starter helpings, use:

> 1 large aubergine (8–10 oz/225–275 g) *or* 10 oz (275 g)
>   round green aubergines
> 1 tablespoon (1 × 15 ml spoon) nut or vegetable oil
> 1 clove garlic, crushed
> ¼ small dried red chilli (to taste), crumbled (optional)
> 1 teaspoon (1 × 5 ml spoon) green curry paste
> 5 fl oz (150 ml) tinned coconut milk
> 4 fl oz (125 ml) chicken stock or water
> 1 spring onion, finely sliced
> 1 teaspoon (1 × 5 ml spoon) fresh root ginger, grated or
>   finely chopped
> 1 kaffir lime leaf, finely chopped with scissors
> ½ teaspoon (½ × 5 ml spoon) palm sugar (or substitute one
>   generous teaspoon thick honey or sugar)
> 5 oz (150 g) Chinese egg noodles or rice sticks
> 2 tablespoons (2 × 15 ml spoons) fresh coriander, chopped
>   (optional)

Cut the aubergine into thick slices, sprinkle with a little salt and leave on a kitchen towel to drain. After 10 minutes turn the slices and leave them for a further 10 minutes. Steam for a few minutes until soft. Cool, then chop coarsely.

Pour the coconut milk into a bowl and beat with a fork or spoon until the creamy part is well integrated with the thinner liquid.

Sauté the garlic, spring onion and chilli (if using) in the oil in the bottom of a medium-sized saucepan over a low heat for just a few seconds. Add the curry paste and continue to stir until mixed together with the oil. Add the steamed and chopped aubergine, then the coconut milk and stock (or water), and stir together well, still over a low flame. Add the ginger, lime leaf and palm sugar, and stir together. Simmer for a minute or two, then stew on a low flame for about 10 minutes, taking care not to let it burn.

At the last moment, cook the Chinese noodles in plenty of salted boiling water for just a couple of minutes, taking great care not to overcook. (If you are using rice sticks, prepare as in the recipe on page 156.) Mix together gently with the sauce on a preheated dish, sprinkle over the chopped coriander, and serve immediately.

Vegetarian red coconut curry, served with noodles

The red curry has a slightly more salty flavour than the green. If you look at the list of ingredients for these two curries in a Thai cook book, you will see that the green is made with green chillis, red with red, but apart from that there seems to be not much difference!

Again, a delicate Thai curry. Goes equally well with noodles or rice.

For 2 light main course helpings, use:

> 1 tablespoon (1 × 15 ml spoon) nut or vegetable oil
> 1 clove garlic, crushed
> ½ small dried red chilli (to taste), crumbled (optional)
> 1 tablespoon (1 × 15 ml spoon) red curry paste
> 8 fl oz (225 ml) tinned coconut milk
> a little water or vegetable stock
> 1 tablespoon (1 × 15 ml spoon) fresh root ginger, grated or finely chopped
> 1 inch (2½ cm) galangal, peeled and sliced into thin rounds
> ½ tablespoon (½ × 15 ml spoon) fish sauce (optional)
> 2 kaffir lime leaves, cut finely using kitchen scissors
> 2 inches (5 cm) lemon grass, finely sliced
> 1 teaspoon (1 × 5 ml spoon) palm sugar (or substitute one generous teaspoon thick honey or sugar)
> 10 oz (275 g) small round green aubergines, halved, *or* 10 oz (275 g) Mediterranean aubergines, thickly sliced, drained (see page 57), slices cut into quarters
> ½ red pepper (or yellow, or green), finely sliced
> 8 oz (225 g) courgettes, sliced
> 5 oz (150 g) Chinese egg noodles

Pour the coconut milk into a bowl and beat with a fork or spoon until the creamy part is well integrated with the thinner liquid. Measure out the 8 fl oz (225 ml).

Sauté the garlic and chilli (if using) in the oil in the bottom of a medium-sized saucepan over a low heat for just a few seconds. Add the curry paste and stir until mixed together with the oil. Add the coconut milk and stir together well, still over a low flame. Add the ginger, galangal, fish sauce (if using), lime leaves, lemon grass and palm sugar, and stir together. Simmer for a minute or two, then add the aubergine and pepper. Cover and simmer for 5 minutes, until the aubergine softens and reduces in volume, then add the courgette. Simmer on a very low heat for another 20 minutes, stirring occasionally and taking care not to let it burn, adding a little stock or water if necessary.

At the last moment, cook the Chinese noodles in plenty of salted boiling water for just a couple of minutes, taking great care not to overcook. Drain, and then mix gently with the sauce on a preheated dish and serve immediately; or serve separately, with the noodles (or rice) on the side.

Spicy Thai spring greens with kaffir lime leaves and coconut milk

You could actually make this recipe with almost any leafy green vegetable – for example Savoy cabbage, spinach or even courgettes. Spring greens, however, have a particularly individual and strong taste which seems to combine well with these other ingredients, and when available they are usually one of the best buys around.

For 2 light main course helpings, use:

10 oz (275 g) spring greens, sliced into medium/fine strips
1½ tablespoons (1½ × 15 ml spoons) nut or vegetable oil
1–2 cloves garlic, crushed
¼ small dried red chilli (to taste), crumbled (optional)
1 large spring onion, finely sliced
1 teaspoon (1 × 5 ml spoon) fresh root ginger, grated or finely chopped
1 large or two small kaffir lime leaves, finely chopped with scissors
½ teaspoon (½ × 5 ml spoon) palm sugar (or substitute one generous teaspoon thick honey or sugar)
1 teaspoon (1 × 5 ml spoon) fish sauce (optional)
2 inches (5 cm) lemon grass, finely sliced
4 fl oz (125 ml) tinned coconut milk
a little stock or water
5 oz (150 g) Chinese egg noodles, buckwheat or 'soba' noodles

Steam or boil the sliced spring greens for a few minutes until softened. Drain. Sauté the garlic, spring onion and chilli (if using) in the oil in the bottom of a medium-sized saucepan over a low flame for just a few seconds. Add the ginger, lime leaf, palm sugar, fish sauce, lemon grass, coconut milk and spring greens, and continue to sauté for about 5 minutes, adding a little vegetable or chicken stock, or water mixed with coconut milk, if the mixture becomes too dry.

At the last moment, cook the Chinese noodles in plenty of salted boiling water for just a couple of minutes, taking great care not to overcook. Drain, and then mix together gently with the sauce on a preheated dish, and serve immediately.

Recipe for béchamel sauce

Béchamel sauce is used in a number of the recipes. To make the sauce, use the quantities specified for the recipe you are following, and proceed as follows:

VERSION 1

Put the milk into a pan with 2 bay leaves, half an onion and a few peppercorns. Bring to just below the boil, then remove from the heat and leave to infuse for 15 minutes. Strain.

Melt the butter slowly in a heavy-bottomed pan, taking care not to let it burn. Mix in the flour, stirring well with a wooden spoon. Add the milk, a little at a time, stirring constantly until the lumps disappear and the sauce thickens. If the sauce ingredients include mustard powder and/or grated cheese, stir them in when you have used up all the milk.

VERSION 2 (A QUICKER METHOD)

If you are in a hurry, proceed as above, but omit the bay leaves, onion and peppercorns and use milk straight from the bottle or carton.

Note: If the sauce develops lumps, beat it with an egg whisk or electric hand beater. I usually whisk it anyway, for good measure!

Index

Main ingredients are indicated by **bold** type

174